FLAVOURS

OF

New Brunswick

FLAVOURS
OF
New Brunswick

The Best Recipes From Our Kitchens

Karen Powell

NIMBUS
PUBLISHING

Nimbus Publishing Limited
3731 Mackintosh St, Halifax, NS, B3K 5A5
(902) 455-4286 nimbus.ca

Printed and bound in Canada
Cover illustrations: iStock, Jenn Embree
Design: Jenn Embree

NB1301

Library and Archives Canada Cataloguing in Publication
Powell, Karen Elaine, 1967-, author
Flavours of New Brunswick : the best recipes from our kitchens /
Karen Powell.
ISBN 978-1-77108-488-8 (softcover)
1. Cooking, Canadian. 2. Cooking, Canadian--Maritime Provinces style. 3.
Cookbooks. I. Title.

TX715.6.P689 2017   641.59715'1   C2016-908041-2

Nimbus Publishing acknowledges the financial support for its publishing activities from the Government of Canada, the Canada Council for the Arts, and from the Province of Nova Scotia. We are pleased to work in partnership with the Province of Nova Scotia to develop and promote our creative industries for the benefit of all Nova Scotians.

I would like to dedicate this "best of" collection to all those who purchased my first two cookbooks and gave me such encouraging praise, kind feedback, and many delightful comments. I frequently heard: "Mmm, that was sooo good"; "that recipe was so easy to make"; "do you have any of those cookies left?" or "can you make me this?"

To those who told others about my recipes and helped create my foodie career here in Saint John, New Brunswick: thank you from the bottom of my heart.

Happy eating!

Contents

• • • • • • • • • • • • • • • •

Author's Note

I am very pleased to present you with the "best of" collection from my two previous cookbooks, *A taste of New Brunswick: recipes from our kitchens* (2001) and *Flavours of New Brunswick: more recipes from our kitchens* (2005). These cookbooks were great successes and sold over 10,000 and 5,000 copies respectively before they were declared "out of print."

The recognition from the local literary community and the general public was beyond rewarding—it was simply sweet. Exceeding "sales by local authors" numbers in my first year was a great accomplishment I will never forget. My first two cookbooks enabled me to grow my reputation in the New Brunswick foodie community. These publications allowed me to expand my catering career, support many local charities through fundraisers and book signings, and partner with various local businesses to help grow and promote New Brunswick's rich food heritage. The kinds words and reams of encouragement from those who bought the books and tried the recipes were sometimes overwhelming, but also kept pushing me onto the path of cooking I knew I was meant to be on.

These cookbooks became my business card. I used them to encourage people to enjoy local ingredients while bringing back memories of families bonding during mealtime, of when food had an impact and accompanied treasured times that turned out to mean so much more than just a meal.

Food is such an important rite of passage, and so many special memories are created during meals or over food served at family events. It is a great accomplishment when we can recreate and share our favourite dishes. Food is even a wonderful tool we can use to explore our diverse history and heritage.

From getting to know our local farmers and buying the perfect ingredients for that special dish, to sharing recipes or replicating dishes made by a family member now passed on, we show what food means to us and the impact it has on our heritage and emotions every time we step into the kitchen.

This book is a collection of my favourite recipes, the recipes from books one and two that customers have told me they enjoyed the most. There is a great selection of recipes celebrating the diverse food growing in our region. I hope you enjoy making and sharing them as much as I have enjoyed sharing them with you.

Staples

Butter and Cream

Butter is the richness that comes from milk but it is really the fat of the milk. Buttermilk is the by-product of churning milk into butter; it is low in fat and very good for cooking.

Commercial buttermilk is made from skim (fat-free) to 3% milk, and thickened naturally through curing.

Butter serves many purposes. It provides a flavour like no other for homemade bread, hot steaming potatoes and vegetables, plus much more. It is also an essential ingredient for pastry cooks.

Clarified Butter is made when you heat unsalted butter slowly over low heat until completely melted. The butter will automatically separate into a clear golden liquid (pure butter fat) and the foamy white additives (milk proteins, water). You then skim off the white foam and discard it. The golden liquid is the clarified butter which contains the full butter flavour you are seeking to add to your dish.

Clarified butter also has a high smoke point, meaning it doesn't burn as easily as regular butter. It can be kept in the fridge for 1 month sealed in a container. You may use butter or margarine anywhere it calls for clarified butter in this book, but you may risk adding more salt or burning your dish, and it may not taste as intended.

Cream is better than butter, according to some cooks, but each has its own place in the kitchen. Cream is high in fat, so if you are watching your fat intake you can reduce the fat content in another part of the recipe, or leave the cream out altogether. The only milk product that doesn't always work as a substitute is skim milk, as it has no fat; this means it has no binding properties to allow thickening to occur.

The higher the fat content, the less you will require in your recipe to add flavour and the quicker your dish will thicken.

Types of Cream: Cream with 35% milk fat is known as whipping cream; cream with 18% milk fat is commonly referred to as coffee cream; cream with 10% milk fat is usually called cereal cream. "Heavy cream" refers to any of the above.

Onions

There are many varieties of onion and each has
its own distinctive taste and use.

- -

Yellow onions are normally yellow in colour and small to medium in size. They are a general-purpose onion with a medium flavour; not too spicy or too sweet.

Spanish onions are yellow and thick-skinned, fairly large in size (usually 4 or more inches in diameter), and have a spicy hotness.

Shallots are small, oval-shaped onions that are best described as a cross between an onion and mild garlic. Shallot skins are thick and more of a darker yellow-orange than most onions. Their flavour is very unique and treasured by many cooks.

White onions peel very easily, as they have a thin papery skin. They taste mild and sweet and are great for eating raw on salads or in sandwiches. They come medium to large in size, but in summertime the baby version is grown specifically for pickling.

Red onions are red and white in colour. They have a tough, bright, deep purplish skin. Once peeled they are very juicy and do bleed their colour a little. If you wish to remove this colour, soak them in a cold-water bath for 20 minutes, then rinse under running water until water runs clear. They are sweet but contain a hot onion bite as well. Great for salads and eating raw. They are medium to large in size and also come in a baby version.

Vidalia onions are sweet, and are medium to large in size, and appear a little flattened instead of perfectly round. The skin is very thin and papery. Their colour varies from pale yellow to cream with darker yellow patches. The sweetness of this onion makes it a delicacy. It is great in pickles, chutneys, and salads. French onion soup made with vidalia onions is out of this world.

Chives are thin, green, hollow shoots of the chive plant, not to be confused with green onions. They produce purple flowers which are also edible. Chives are very strong in flavour with an earthy but savoury onion flavour.

Green onions are small-to-medium-sized tubes with green tops and white bottoms. They are used in Mexican, Japanese, and Chinese cooking frequently. They are mild in flavour, but strong in smell.

Leeks are very mild and smooth-tasting. They look a bit like jumbo, flattened green onions, and are usually between 18 inches and 2 to 3 feet long. They are pale green on top and white near the bottom. They taste like a cross between a mild onion, mild garlic, and celery. Leeks taste great in soups and chowders and are perfect on pizza. Commonly used in French cuisine, leeks are often paired with salmon.

Spring onions look like thick green onions and have medium-sized white bulbs at the bottom of long, hollow, dark-green shoots. They are very strong with a medium bite.

Shop around your local grocery store or farmers' market for varieties to try!

Fundy Fog Pea Soup

This soup is a staple in Maritime kitchens; it is a traditional favourite for a wintery Saturday supper after an afternoon on a frozen river.

Method

1. Combine all ingredients in a large stock pot and simmer over low to medium heat until peas are dissolved. Approximately 2 hours.

2. If you like a full-bodied soup you can add diced carrot, turnip, or even potatoes. About 1 cup of each would suffice. Add in the final hour of cooking time.

3. Serve piping hot.

Ingredients

› 2 cups split peas (green or yellow), uncooked

› ¾ cup onion, minced

› 6 cups water or chicken stock

› 1 tablespoon soya sauce

› 1 cup ham pieces (and ham bone, if available)

› salt and pepper to taste

Optional add-in

› dumplings or dough boys*

Dumplings may be cooked directly in the soup during the last 20–30 minutes before serving. Try the recipe on page 141.

Work up an appetite at Fundy National Park. With 100 kilometres of walking trails and fabulous scenery, it is a jewel in New Brunswick's crown of beautiful destinations. The Bay of Fundy also boasts the world's highest tides.

Springtime Tomato Basil Soup

This is the perfect lunch after a morning spent in the garden. If you still have some tomatoes preserved from last year's bounty, use them to remind you of what is to come.

Ingredients

- 1 cup onion, diced

- 1 cup mushrooms, sliced

- 1 cup celery, diced

- 1 cup green pepper, diced

- 1 cup carrots, diced

- 1 tablespoon garlic, minced

- 2 tablespoons dried basil

- 1 teaspoon dried oregano

- 3 cups crushed tomatoes

- 1 (15 ounce) can tomato paste

- 3–5 cups stock

- 1 teaspoon white pepper

- salt to taste

Method

1. Place all of the ingredients in a large stock pot. Add enough stock to cover vegetables by 2 inches.

2. Simmer 1 hour on low heat, stirring occasionally.

3. Serve piping hot.

Winter Corn Chowder

This heartwarming soup combined with a green salad and crusty bread makes a filling, delicious, balanced meal.

Method

1. In a large pot, melt butter and brown the onion and garlic until fragrant, about 3 minutes.

2. Add the rest of the ingredients and cook over low heat for 1 hour, or until potatoes are tender.

3. Serve piping hot.

Serves 4–6

Ingredients

- 2 tablespoons butter

- ½ cup onion, minced

- 1 clove garlic, minced

- 2 cups evaporated milk

- 1 cup condensed cream of chicken soup

- 3 cups vegetable or chicken stock

- 2 cups potatoes, peeled and cubed

- ½ cup celery, diced

- ½ cup green pepper, diced

- 3 cups corn (whole or cream)

- 1 tablespoon soya sauce

- salt and pepper to taste

Spicy Sweet Potato Soup

Ingredients

- 8 large sweet potatoes (or approximately 5 pounds)

- 2 apples (sweet variety like Honeycrisp works best)

- 16 cups chicken stock

- 1 cup evaporated milk

- zest of 1 lemon

- 1 tablespoon Worcestershire sauce

- 1 tablespoon fresh ginger root, grated

- ½ cup lemon juice

- ½ teaspoon hot pepper flakes

- 1 tablespoon soya sauce

- salt and pepper to taste

Method

1. Peel, rinse, and cube sweet potatoes into 1-inch pieces.

2. Peel, core, and mince apples.

3. In a large pot, boil potatoes and apples in the stock until they are very soft, about 20 minutes. Drain, making sure to reserve all liquid in a separate bowl.

4. Mash the potatoes and apples thoroughly with a potato masher or blend with a hand-held mixer on low speed for 2 to 3 minutes until smooth.

5. Gradually add milk and some of the reserved stock until desired soup consistency is reached.

6. Add zest, Worcestershire sauce, ginger, lemon juice, pepper flakes, soya sauce, salt and pepper.

7. Blend for 2 additional minutes. Serve hot with crusty bread or dumplings.

Serves 4–8

Acadian Chicken Fricot a.k.a. Fricot au poulet

Often served with dumplings, this traditional Acadian stew is the ultimate comfort food. A good homemade stock is the key!

Method

1. Place all ingredients into a deep pot, and simmer over medium heat until potatoes are tender.

Suggestion: Add some dumplings made with a little summer savoury, sage, or poultry seasoning in the last 10 minutes of cooking. (Try the recipe on page 141.)

Serves 4–10

*If you cook a roast chicken dinner for the family one Sunday, save the carcass and pull some white meat off to use in your fricot. If desired, roast a chicken just for this recipe, which will produce a more full-bodied stew.

Ingredients

- 8 cups chicken broth

- 2 cups shredded chicken (best pulled from a roasted chicken*)

- 1 cup onion, sliced round

- 2 cups cabbage, roughly chopped into medium-sized pieces

- 1 cup carrots, peeled and thinly sliced

- 3 cups potatoes, peeled and cut into chunks

- ½ cup mushrooms, thinly sliced

- ½ teaspoon summer savoury

- ½ teaspoon oregano

- 1 tablespoon soya sauce

- 1 tablespoon Worcestershire sauce

Chicken and Greens Soup

Try adding some savoury dumplings or rice to this soup for a little variety.

Ingredients

- 1 tablespoon butter

- 1 cup onion, finely minced

- 1 cup mushrooms, thinly sliced

- 4 cups greens*

- 8 litres chicken broth

- 1 tablespoon soya sauce

- 1 tablespoon Worcestershire sauce

- ¼ cup white sugar

- ½ teaspoon dried dill

- 1 bay leaf

- salt and pepper to taste

Any combination of fava beans, sugar snap peas, snow peas, asparagus, fiddleheads, garden peas, collard greens, spinach, or string beans would work.

Method

1. In a deep pot, melt the butter and sauté the onion and mushrooms. Add all the greens and sauté for and additional 3 minutes on high, stirring constantly.

2. Add all remaining ingredients to the pot and bring to a boil.

3. Reduce heat to low. Simmer until greens are tender, approximately 5 to 10 minutes.

4. Serve piping hot with a dollop of sour cream in the middle and crusty bread on the side

Note: Use a stainless steel or any non-reactive pot, otherwise the greens may turn grey, blacken, or become bitter.

Serves 4–6

Good Old Hamburger Stew

Method

1. Brown beef in a large stock pot. Drain fat.

2. Place everything except potatoes in pot, cover, and let simmer on low heat, stirring often, for 1 hour.

3. Add potatoes and cook for 30 minutes more.

4. Serve piping hot.

Gardeners and lovers of flowers and fauna will enjoy a stroll through the Kingsbrae Gardens in St. Andrews. The 27 acres offer something for everyone, from roses to heather to butterfly bushes.

Ingredients

> 1 pound ground beef

> 3 cups beef stock

> 2 cups carrots, chopped

> 1 cup onion, chopped

> 1 cup mushrooms, sliced

> 1 cup green pepper, diced

> ½ cup celery, chopped

> 4 cups stewed tomatoes, chopped

> ½ cup tomato paste

> 1 can condensed tomato soup

> 1 tablespoon garlic, minced

> 1 tablespoon dried basil

> 1 teaspoon dried mint

> 1 teaspoon dried oregano

> 1 large bay leaf

> 2 cups potatoes, peeled and diced

SOUPS

Warm Field Tomato Salad

Use this recipe as a tasty side dish, or as a base for veggie pizza.
You could also toss it with pasta or rice for a full meal.

Ingredients

> ¼ cup olive oil

> 2 pounds tomatoes*

> ¼ cup onion, finely minced

> ¼ cup celery, finely minced

> 1 pound green beans, sliced thinly

> 2 cloves garlic, minced

Use fresh garden tomato varieties like yellow, orange, heirloom, cherry, grape, or plum.

Method

1. Heat oil over low heat. Add remaining ingredients and sauté for 5 minutes, or until beans are tender.

Serves 4–6

Did you know? The crossword was originally invented by Edward McDonald from Shediac in 1926. It started out like a very prehistoric version of Scrabble. Board games and puzzles are a great way to pass the hot summer days sipping punch on the beach or at a barbecue.

Chicken Caesar Salad

Method

1. Grill chicken, and season with salt and pepper. Let cool, then cut into bite-sized strips.

2. Place lettuce and chicken in a large salad bowl and set aside.

3. In a small bowl, mix lemon juice, vinegar, garlic, and oregano.

4. Pour dressing over top of salad, toss until chicken and lettuce are coated, and serve immediately.

5. Sprinkle with Parmesan cheese.

Salad

> 2 large boneless, skinless chicken breasts

> 1 head romaine lettuce, cut into bite-sized pieces

> salt and pepper to taste

Dressing

> ½ cup lemon juice

> ½ cup apple cider vinegar

> 2 tablespoon garlic, minced

> 1 teaspoon dried oregano

> shaved Parmesan cheese to garnish

Sweet Crunchy Salad

Salad

- 2 cups red cabbage

- 1 cup Granny Smith apple

- ½ a red onion

- 1 cup fresh cranberries

- ½ cup pecans, chopped

- ½ cup walnuts, chopped

Dressing

- ¼ cup olive oil

- 1 tablespoon soya sauce

- 1 tablespoon Worcestershire sauce

- ¼ cup prepared mustard

- ¼ cup honey

Method

1. Grate cabbage, apple, and onion. Place into a deep mixing bowl.

2. Cut cranberries in half and add to bowl. Add nuts and set aside.

3. In a smaller bowl, make the dressing. Mix the olive oil, soya sauce, Worcestershire sauce, mustard, and honey. Whisk until mixture is smooth and even.

4. Drizzle dressing on salad, toss to coat, and serve immediately.

Serves 4–8

Warm Summer Spinach Salad

Method

1. Prepare rice according to package directions. Cool rice, fluff with a fork, and set aside.

2. Rinse spinach and tear into bite-sized pieces.

3. Place spinach in a deep bowl, add rice and toss. Set aside.

4. Fry bacon until crispy. Drain off grease, but reserve 1 tablespoon.

5. Break bacon into small pieces. Sprinkle bacon into spinach and rice mixture.

6. Using the reserved 1 tablespoon of bacon grease, fry the onion and mushrooms until golden. Sprinkle with salt and pepper.

7. Toss the hot onions and mushrooms with the spinach mixture.

8. Drizzle balsamic vinegar over salad, toss again, and serve immediately.

Serves 4–10

Ingredients

> 1 cup wild rice, uncooked

> 2 pounds fresh baby spinach

> ½ pound bacon, uncooked

> 1 cup sweet onion, minced

> 2 cups mushrooms, sliced thin

> salt and pepper to taste

> ¼ cup balsamic vinegar

Creamy Fiddlehead and Cheese Casserole

Ingredients

> 3 pounds fresh fiddleheads

> 1 recipe thin béchamel sauce (page 113)

> ½ cup lemon juice

> zest of 1 lemon

> ¼ cup Parmesan cheese, grated

> ¼ cup mozzarella cheese, grated

> 1 tablespoon Worcestershire sauce

> 1 tablespoon soya sauce

> salt and pepper to taste

> 1 cup dry bread crumbs

Method

1. Preheat oven to 325°. Clean fiddleheads thoroughly and place in a shallow baking dish. Set aside.

2. Prepare béchamel sauce as per instructions. Remove from heat.

3. To the béchamel sauce add lemon juice, zest, cheeses, Worcestershire sauce, soya sauce, salt and pepper. Whisk until smooth.

4. Pour sauce over fiddleheads.

5. Sprinkle bread crumbs over top.

6. Bake until bubbly and golden, approximately 30 minutes.

Serves 6–10

Coq au Vin

Method

1. Preheat oven to 325°.

2. Cook bacon bits in oven-safe frying pan. Remove bits but reserve grease. Add butter and chicken, frying over medium to high heat until browned.

3. Add all remaining ingredients plus the bacon to the frying pan and bake uncovered for 45 to 90 minutes, or until sauce starts to thicken and chicken falls off the bone.

Suggestion: Serve piping hot with bread for dipping, or over a bed of mashed potatoes.

Serves 4–8

Ingredients

- 4 slices bacon, diced

- ¼ cup clarified butter (recipe on page 2)

- 3 pounds bone-in chicken

- 2 cups onion, minced

- 3 cups potatoes, peeled and diced

- 1 cup mushrooms, sliced

- 1 cup carrots, grated

- 1 clove garlic, minced

- 2 bay leaves

- 1 teaspoon dried thyme

- 1 teaspoon dried parsley

- 1 cup red wine

- 1 to 3 litres chicken stock to cover

- salt and pepper to taste

Corned Beef Pie

Remember to hide the salt shaker when you serve this meal! Early settlers in New Brunswick relied on salt to cure meat and fish to preserve it.

Ingredients

- 2 pounds canned corned beef

- ½ cup onion, minced

- 1 tablespoon soya sauce

- 2 cups beef or chicken stock

- pepper to taste

- 2 Perfect Pie Crust (recipe on page 176)

- 3 cups mashed potatoes

Optional add-ins

- ½ cup mushrooms, sliced

- ½ cup green pepper, diced

- 2 cups assorted vegetables (corn, peas, carrots), diced

Method

1. Remove fat from beef, and break the meat into small chunks. Place in a deep pot with onion, soya sauce, and stock. Simmer on low heat for 20 minutes.

2. Preheat oven to 350° while the mixture simmers.

3. Continue to cook until mixture is as thick as oatmeal. Add mushrooms or green peppers to corned beef mixture (if desired). Set aside to cool.

4. Place the bottom crust in a deep pie pan and build pie in layers: corned beef mixture, assorted vegetables (if desired), then mashed potatoes. Repeat layers until all ingredients are used.

5. Place top crust over everything, then press top and bottom edges together. Pierce top of pie with a fork to allow venting.

6. Bake for 30–50 minutes, or until crust is golden and juices are bubbling.

Garden Vegetable Linguine

Method

1. Prepare pasta according to package directions.

2. Meanwhile, melt butter over high heat and sauté all of the vegetables until tender, approximately 3 to 5 minutes.

3. Add garlic, Worcestershire sauce, soya sauce, oregano, basil, sugar, salt, and pepper.

4. Continue to cook and stir gently until heated through.

5. Toss vegetables with pasta and serve immediately.

Serves 4–8

Ingredients

> 1 (400-gram) package linguine

> 1 tablespoon clarified butter (recipe on page 2)

> 1 cup zucchini, julienned with peel on

> ½ cup snow peas, julienned

> 1 red pepper, julienned

> 1 cup carrots, julienned

> ½ cup green onion, diced

> 1 cup plum tomatoes, diced

> 2 cloves garlic, minced

> 1 tablespoon Worcestershire sauce

> 1 tablespoon soya sauce

> 1 teaspoon dried oregano

> 1 teaspoon dried basil

> 1 teaspoon white sugar

> salt and pepper to taste

MAINS

Saturday Meatloaf

Loaf

> 3 pounds lean ground beef

> 2 cups bread crumbs

> 1 can condensed cream of mushroom soup

> 2 eggs, beaten

> 1 cup onion, minced

> 1 teaspoon garlic, minced

> ¼ teaspoon dried mint

> salt and pepper to taste

Sauce

> 1 cup ketchup

> 1 cup brown sugar

> 2 tablespoons prepared mustard

Method

1. Preheat oven to 350°.

2. In a large bowl combine bread crumbs, cream of mushroom soup, eggs, onion, garlic, mint, salt, and pepper until the bread crumbs are wet.

3. Add ground beef and mix evenly.

4. Press mixture into a loaf pan and bake for 1 hour. Drain grease.

5. In a small bowl, mix ketchup, brown sugar, and mustard. Pour over meatloaf and return to oven for 20 minutes.

Hint: For easier serving portions and shorter cooking time, use a muffin tin to create individual loaves. Reduce cooking time by half, then check with meat thermometer to ensure meat has reached 160°.

Sunday Roast Beef and Vegetables

Save the drippings from your roast and try the Traditional Yorkshire Pudding recipe on page 144.

Method

1. Preheat oven to 300°.

2. In a large roasting pan, place roast with 4 cups broth and 2 cups water. Cover and bake for 1 hour without opening oven door.

3. Check roast, turn heat up to 475°, and brown roast all over, (approximately 20 minutes per pound). Let roast get crispy all over but do not let the pan dry out.

4. Add remaining 8 cups of broth, 1 cup of water, and all other ingredients. Stir.

5. Cover and bake at 350° until vegetables are tender, about 30 to 90 minutes, depending on size.

Suggestion: Thicken pan drippings with flour and water to make gravy or serve your roast stew-style.

Serves 4–8

Ingredients

- 5 to 8 pounds beef (sirloin, striploin, or T-bone)

- 12 cups beef broth

- 3 cups water

- 3 cups onion, cut into medium-sized chunks

- 1 cup mushrooms, halved

- 1 pound baby carrots

- 3 pounds potatoes

- 1 tablespoon soya sauce

- 1 tablespoon Worcestershire sauce

Tourtière

Ingredients

- 1 tablespoon olive oil

- 2 pounds pork, dark meat

- 1 cup onion, minced

- 1 clove garlic, minced

- ½ teaspoon fresh ginger root, grated (or ¼ teaspoon powdered ginger)

- 1 cup mushrooms, sliced

- ½ teaspoon dried rosemary

- 2 cups beef broth

- 1 tablespoon Worcestershire sauce

- 1 tablespoon soya sauce

- 1 double layer Savoury Pie Crust (recipe on page 177)

- 1 tablespoon cornstarch

- salt and pepper to taste

- ½ cup mashed potatoes

Method

1. Heat oil in a shallow frying pan over medium to high heat. Fry pork until it is browned and caramelized. The meat should look almost burnt with residue stuck to the bottom of the pan.

2. Reduce heat to low, remove meat, and set it aside.

3. Fry onion in same pan for a few minutes, scraping up the brown bits stuck to the pan with your spatula.

4. Add garlic, ginger, mushrooms, and rosemary, and fry for about 5 minutes until mushrooms are soft.

5. Add broth, Worcestershire sauce, and soya sauce, and return meat to pan. Cover tightly and simmer over low heat until meat falls apart easily, adding more broth or water as needed. Meat must not dry out and you must end up with at least 2 cups finished broth. (Approximately 30 minutes to 2 hours, depending.)

6. Preheat oven to 375°.

Continued next page...

7. Cool mixture and shred meat into strings or small bite-sized pieces. Discard any fat, gristle, or bones.

8. Place the bottom pie shell in a greased pie plate, and then pour in meat mixture and broth.

9. Sprinkle cornstarch and salt and pepper evenly over meat mixture.

10. Spread the entire pie with a thin layer of mashed potatoes.

11. Add top pie crust, squeezing together the edges of the two crusts. Use a fork to pierce a few vent holes in the top layer.

12. Bake until crust is golden and juices are bubbly.

Makes 1 (9-inch) pie

Full Meal Deal Skewers

Ingredients

- 1 pound small potatoes (new, red- and/or white-skinned)
- 8 to 10 bamboo skewers
- 1 pound boneless chicken breast
- 1 pound pork
- 1 pound beef
- 1 pound medium sized shrimp cleaned, de-veined
- 1 pound corn on the cob
- 1 pound zucchini
- 1 pound green pepper
- 1 pound red pepper
- 1 pound sweet onions
- 1 pound small whole mushrooms
- 2 cups Italian-style salad dressing

Method

1. Parboil potatoes for 5 minutes in salted water.

2. Cut the vegetables into 1-inch pieces and the meat into 1-inch cubes. Make sure all pieces are the same size so they cook evenly. The bigger the pieces, the longer they will take to cook.

3. Thread food on skewers starting with a vegetable, then a piece of meat or seafood, then another vegetable, making sure each skewer has one of each of the items (or whatever combo you like).

4. Place skewers in a shallow baking pan and coat with salad dressing. Cover and refrigerate for 15 minutes.

5. Remove skewers from marinade.

6. Place skewers directly on barbecue or in the oven at 375° on a cookie sheet.

7. Baste with marinade as they cook.

8. Cook until shrimp are pink and curled tightly, approximately 10 to 20 minutes.

Serves 4–10

Fresh Garden Vegetable Stirfry

Method

1. In a large frying pan, melt butter and oil over low heat.

2. Increase heat to medium-high.

3. Add carrots and chickpeas. Fry for 2 minutes, stirring constantly.

4. Add the onion, peas, and mushrooms, and fry for 5 minutes stirring often.

5. Add asparagus, garlic, sugar, Worcestershire sauce, soya sauce, lemon juice, and parsley. Continue to fry for 3 minutes, stirring often.

6. Serve over a bed of rice or noodles, or as a side dish.

Serves 4–10

Ingredients

> 2 tablespoons butter

> 1 teaspoon olive oil

> 1 cup carrots, peeled and sliced

> 1 (19-ounce) can chickpeas, drained

> 1 cup red onion, diced

> 1 cup fresh garden peas

> 1 cup mushrooms, sliced

> 1 cup asparagus tips

> 1 clove garlic, minced

> 1 tablespoon white sugar

> 1 tablespoon Worcestershire sauce

> 1 tablespoon soya sauce

> 1 tablespoon lemon juice

> 1 tablespoon fresh parsley, chopped

MAINS

Rappie Pie
a.k.a. Pâté à la râpure

Ingredients

- 2 pounds bone-in chicken

- 1 cup onion, chopped

- 1 cup carrots, peeled and chopped

- 1 cup celery, chopped

- 2 bay leaves

- 5 pounds starchy* potatoes, peeled and grated

- ½ pound pork fat, diced small

- 8 to 16 cups broth**

- salt and pepper to taste

Method

1. Preheat oven to 350°

2. Bake chicken with onions, carrots, celery, and bay leaves until fully cooked and falling off the bone, about 1 hour. Discard bay leaves. Let cool, then remove all bones and non-edible matter and discard. Set meat and vegetables aside in a bowl.

3. Pour 1 cup broth into the bottom of a casserole dish. Next, place a layer of meat and vegetables, followed by a layer of potatoes, and repeat until you end up with potatoes on top.

4. Sprinkle with cubes of pork fat, spaced as evenly as possible. Bake at 350° for 30 to 90 minutes based on the thickness of your pan. The top will be golden brown and the juices from inside will be bubbling up.

Serves 6–12 (makes one 9 x 13 pan)

Continued next page...

Potatoes are best stored between 7 to 10 degrees Celsius. Keep them in a dark place to prevent sprouting. Remove them from plastic bags if you buy them this way as they will sweat and rot quicker. Exposure to light may turn them green and they sometimes become bitter. If you store them too cold they will get grey spots; they are still okay to eat but will discolour as they cook (becoming greyer) and their taste may change.

Named from the French "*patates râpées*," meaning "grated potatoes," the popularity of rappie pie increased when women discovered that the water squeezed from the potatoes was very high in starch. This liquid filled the need for starch in the laundry room. They then added the broth back into the potatoes and layered the potatoes in deep casserole dishes with mounds of meat and sometimes vegetables. The top was then covered with little cubes of port fat, which help form a crispy, flavourful crust and filled the houses with a delicious smell.

Traditionally, the meat used was rabbit, but it was soon replaced with any meat on hand; chicken has became the favourite in the recent years. Sometimes it is made with seafood like clams or scallops. It continues to be a popular dish today; you can even purchase grated potatoes specially made for rappie pie. Check with your local grocer.

Staples

*The potatoes must be the starchiest variety you can find to produce the best results (red- or yellow-skinned, Yukon gold, or russets to name a few). Start by grating the peeled raw potatoes into a deep bowl. You will notice they produce a lot of juice, which is very starchy. Place the potatoes in a cheesecloth or another cloth bag strong enough to withstand your attempts to remove all liquids. You can mash the cloth or bag with a potato masher, hang it up to drip, squeeze it by hand, or squish it with a heavy object over a drain. The goal is to remove as much of the liquid from the grated potatoes as possible. Discard the liquid.

**You will be rehydrating these grated potatoes with a very flavourful broth. The broth must be the best flavour you can produce for this dish to turn out just like Grandma used to make. Place the grated and drained potatoes into a deep bowl or pot and slowly add broth until you reach the consistency of mashed potatoes—no heat required. You will then layer the potato mixture with meat and or vegetables into a deep casserole dish.

Maple-Glazed Chicken

This glaze is delicious on ribs, pork, and fish too!

Chicken

- 2 pounds chicken pieces of choice

Glaze

- 1 cup maple syrup
- 2 cups water
- 3 cloves garlic, minced
- ¼ cup soya sauce
- 1 tablespoon butter
- salt and pepper to taste

Method

1. If your chicken is bone-in, parboil the pieces to reduce the overall cooking time, tenderize the meat, and remove most of the fat content.

2. Combine all glaze ingredients in a small pot and bring to a slow boil over medium heat.

3. Thicken the glaze if desired. (Mix 1 tablespoon cornstarch with 2 tablespoons water and add to glaze. Heat until thickened.) Pour over chicken.

4. Transfer chicken pieces to the grill and baste constantly with the glaze. Dip whole pieces in sauce every 5 to 10 minutes and return to grill. Alternatively, bake at 325° for 45 to 90 minutes, or until chicken is thoroughly cooked, basting often.

Tomato Cheese Melt

Method

1. Spread 1 teaspoon of either mayonnaise, ranch dressing, or herbed cream cheese on each piece of bread.

2. Top one slice of bread with the tomatoes. Sprinkle with salt and pepper.

3. Sprinkle cheese on top of the tomatoes.

4. Top with other slice of bread.

5. Fry, grill, or broil until bread is crispy and cheese is melted.

Ingredients

› 2 slices of bread or 2 flour tortillas

› 2 teaspoons mayonnaise, ranch salad dressing, or herbed cream cheese

› 4 slices tomato (very ripe or green tomatoes)

› ¼ cup cheddar* cheese, grated

› salt and pepper to taste

Use a flavour of cheese you like if cheddar is not your favourite: Swiss, blue, mozzarella, havarti, etc.

Summer Greens and Bacon Sauté

Ingredients

- ¼ pound bacon or pancetta*

- 1 teaspoon clarified butter (recipe on page 2)

- 2 pounds greens of choice**

- 1 tablespoon lemon juice

- 1 tablespoon lemon zest

- ½ cup onion, minced

- salt and pepper to taste

Pancetta is Italian bacon that has been cured in salt and spices, then air-dried (not smoked like bacon). Found in many delicatessens.

**Use any greens available such as spinach, asparagus, fiddleheads, or Brussels sprouts. If using Brussels sprouts, you may need to parboil them first if they are tough or large in size.*

Method

1. Fry bacon until crispy, reserve 1 tablespoon of the grease.

2. Pat bacon dry, crumble it, and set aside.

3. Add butter and reserved bacon grease to a stainless steel frying pan and fry greens until they are two-thirds cooked.

4. Add lemon juice, lemon zest, onion, and fry until greens start to turn golden on the edges.

5. Sprinkle with salt and pepper and serve piping hot.

Serves 4–8

Cranberry Baked Beans

Method

1. Melt butter in a large pot over medium heat.

2. Add onion and garlic, fry for 3 to 5 minutes until soft and fragrant.

3. Reduce heat to low and add beans, cranberries, brown sugar, Worcestershire sauce, soya sauce, mustard, and salt and pepper.

4. Stir well so all ingredients are evenly mixed.

5. Simmer on low heat for 15 minutes.

6. Serve with tea biscuits, crusty bread, pastry, or Dough Boys stewed in with the beans during the last 10 minutes of cooking. (See recipe on page 141.)

Serves 4–6

Ingredients

› 1 teaspoon butter

› 1 cup onion, finely minced

› 2 cloves garlic, minced

› 3 (15-ounce) cans ready-to-serve beans in tomato sauce

› 1 cup cranberries*

› ½ cup light brown sugar

› 1 tablespoon Worcestershire sauce

› 1 tablespoon soya sauce

› 1 tablespoon mustard

› salt and pepper to taste

*Can be freshly mashed, jam, jelly, or frozen (thaw first). For a variation try blueberries, raspberries, strawberreis, blackberries, or even diced apples.

Maple Breakfast Tart

Ingredients

> 2 pounds bacon

> 1 Perfect Pie Crust, single layer only (recipe on page 176)

> 1 cup Harvest Time Applesauce (recipe on page 168)

> ½ cup maple syrup

> 1 Crumble Mixture (recipe on page 173)

Method

1. Preheat oven to 425°.

2. Fry bacon until it is three-quarters cooked. Drain fat and crumble bacon into small pieces.

3. Place a single pie shell into a greased pie plate.

4. Spread applesauce, then bacon bits, and then maple syrup over the pie crust. Sprinkle crumble mixture on top.

5. Bake until crumble is toasted and golden.

Suggestion: Serve with a wedge of cheddar cheese or drizzle cheese sauce over top, or add a side dish of fluffy scrambled eggs.

Serves 4–10

Maple sugar shacks dot the winter wonderlands of New Brunswick. Take a tour, pour some sap, collect it, cook it, and take home some sugar pie or freshly made snow candy.

Chicken Donair For One

Method

1. Slice chicken thinly and fry for 1 minute in oil.

2. Add all mushrooms, onions, and peppers and cover pan with lid. Let fry for 2–3 minutes. Uncover and stir until chicken is fully cooked (about 4 more minutes). Sprinkle with salt and pepper.

3. Spoon mixture onto a warmed pita or tortilla, and serve with donair, tzatziki, or ranch sauce. Sprinkle with almonds.

Ingredients

> 1 boneless, skinless chicken breast, uncooked

> ½ teaspoon oil

> ½ cup mushrooms, sliced

> ¼ cup onion, sliced

> ¼ cup green pepper, sliced

> salt and pepper to taste

> pita or tortilla

> sauce of choice (donair, cucumber-yogurt [tzatziki], or ranch)

> 1 tablespoon sliced almonds (optional)

Sautéed Spring Vegetables

Ingredients

- 2 tablespoons butter

- ½ cup onion, finely minced

- 1 cup pecans, chopped

- 1 cup asparagus, cut into 1-inch pieces

- 2 cups fresh fiddleheads, cut into 1-inch pieces

- 1 cup sugar snap peas or large sweet peas

- 2 tablespoons brown sugar

- 2 cups baby spinach

- salt and pepper to taste

Method

1. In a large stainless steel* frying pan, melt butter over medium heat. Add onion and fry for 2 minutes, then add pecans and fry for 1 more minute. Remove from pan and set aside.

2. In the same pan add asparagus, fiddleheads, and peas. Sprinkle with sugar and fry until vegetables are al dente, about 3 to 5 minutes.

3. Add spinach and cook until it starts to wilt. Return the onion and pecans to the pan. Fry for 3 minutes more.

Do not use aluminum or cast iron frying pans, as these will darken or grey the greens. Use stainless steel, ceramic, or glass only.

Serves 4–6

Grilled Portobello Mushrooms

Steak, mushrooms, and a little red wine finish off an idyllic day at the beach.

Method

1. Clean mushrooms and cut into 1-inch-thick slices. Set aside.

2. Whisk together olive oil, garlic, pepper, salt, lemon juice, and tarragon. Pour marinade over mushrooms, cover, and let stand for 10 minutes.

3. Remove mushrooms from marinade and grill for 15 minutes, flipping once. Baste with leftover marinade as they cook.

Ingredients

> 4 portobello mushrooms

> ½ cup olive oil

> 2 tablespoon garlic, minced

> 1 tablespoon black peppercorns, cracked

> ½ teaspoon salt

> ¼ cup lemon juice

> ¼ teaspoon dried tarragon

From the Sea

Shrimp

How to select, clean, store, and prepare

• •

Buying: Shrimp are sold according to their size or count, which is based on the average number of shrimp per pound. The smaller the number, the larger the shrimp, thus resulting in fewer shrimp per pound. Large-variety shrimp are size 4, which represents 4 shrimp to a pound. The smallest may be size 160 or 160 shrimp per pound.

There are more than 300 varieties of shrimp such as brown, pink, blue, white, tiger, and jumbo. Most fishers will tell you that the colder the water, the smaller and more succulent the shrimp. An average size at most fish mongers would be 20 to 40 count; they are great for an all-around flavour, and ease of preparation.

When buying shrimp, trust your nose. Shrimp should never smell fishy, nor should they smell like ammonia. An iodine aroma does not indicate spoilage, but rather the iodine-rich kelp diet of some varieties. Like most seafood, shrimp should smell of salt water and nothing else. In terms of texture, look for firm shrimp that are moist but not slimy, with shiny, flexible-looking shells. If time and energy permit, avoid buying pre-peeled and de-veined shrimp, as cleaning before freezing can diminish their flavour.

Finally, avoid shrimp that have black spots on their shells which is an indication that the shrimp have begun to deteriorate, (with exception of the tiger variety which may contain spots as part of their natural colouring).

Cleaning: Start by pinching off the short legs along the belly of the curled part of the shrimp. Peel off the shell by placing one thumb on either side of the belly where you removed the legs, and pull in an outward motion, starting at the thicker end moving down toward the tail. The tail can be left on (just the last segment) if shrimp will be served as a finger food, thus acting as a handle for the person devouring them. Sometimes shrimp come with their heads still on. They are very easy to remove: grab the head with one hand and bend sideways and it will snap off where it naturally joins the body. Save the heads for stock. Some cooks prefer to cook with heads as they say they contain lots of great flavour.

After you have the shells removed, rinse quickly in cold water. Then with a sharp thin knife slice the shrimp along the backside where the shrimp bends; you will see a dark line just hiding underneath the surface: this is the digestive tract of the shrimp. With your knife gently hook the black line and remove it using cold running water and/or your hands. Discard this black line matter as it may contain sand or other inedible matter. If the shrimp is tiny you may not need to do this as the black line with be too small to remove, thus not affecting flavour at all.

Storing: Store shrimp in your fridge for up to 3 days if they are raw, and 5 days once cooked. Raw shrimp can also be stored in the freezer for up to 12 months.

Cooking: A variety of methods may be used to cook your shrimp, depending on the texture and flavour you're after. Steam for 5 to 20 minutes depending on heat source.

Bake, grill, or pan fry until shrimp are curled tight and pink in colour, approximately 5 to 10 minutes over medium to high heat.

If you are making a soup or sauce with your shrimp, you may boil the leftover shells for 10 minutes in rapidly boiling water with some salt for a flavourful broth, or try my Simple Seafood Broth (recipe on page 55).

Another technique is to butterfly the shrimp, which means to cut them open along the backside. After you have cleaned them, score them a little deeper than you would to remove the black line you normally see there, enough to cut into the shrimp by one-third of its width. This is mainly for larger shrimp where a fancy presentation is preferred. When the shrimp cooks, the edges of the cut you made curl outward thus looking similar to a butterfly with open wings, hence the name. This curling also allows for more flesh to be exposed and creates a sort of well along the centre for sauces to collect.

Mussels

How to select, clean, store, and prepare

· ·

Serving size per person (in the shell):

> ½ to 1 pound as an hors d'oeuvre

> 1 pound as a side dish

> 2 to 3 pounds as a main meal

Storing: Store mussels in the fridge in a shallow pan or bowl covered with a wet cloth. DO NOT ADD TAP WATER to the mussels as this will kill them. Mussels will keep in your fridge for 2 to 3 days.

Buying: Select clean-looking mussels with the shell on. When displayed on ice, the shells should be closed to indicate live and active mussels. Purchase as fresh as possible from a reputable fish monger. Make sure your fish monger puts air in the bag for the trip home as mussels need air to stay alive. Mussels usually sit partially open when out of water. If a mussel's shell is open, gently tap it on the countertop to see if it closes. If the shell does not close, the mussel is dead and not suitable for eating; it must be discarded.

You can also harvest your own wild mussels! Local beaches have seasons that are best and safest for digging, so check with your local department of fisheries for the best times to go.

Cleaning: mussels may come fairly clean (especially the cultivated ones) but often there is still some sand inside and woolly-looking hairs called "beards" still attached to the outside of the shells. Scrub shells with a brush to remove any dirt. Pull off all beards. Quickly rinse shells under tap water being careful not to soak them.

If you prefer to remove mussels from shells before cooking, you will have to force open the shell with a shucking knife available at your fish market. The juice inside the shell is very flavourful so try to shuck cleaned mussels over a bowl to preserve it. Mussels in the shell add a decorative look to seafood dishes.

Cooking: A variety of methods may be used depending on the texture and flavour you're after. Try steaming mussels for between 5 and 20 minutes, depending on heat source. Bake in oven or on barbecue until they pop open, approximately 10 minutes at 425°.

After cooking, all mussel shells should open up. Discard any that do not open up during cooking; they are not safe to eat. If you are making a soup or sauce with your mussels, you may boil the leftover shells for 10 minutes in rapidly boiling water with salt for flavourful broth or see my Simple Seafood Broth recipe on page 55.

Mussels live along coastlines and river mouths. They attach themselves with their thread-like beards to rocks, wharf pilings, or other saltwater-submerged surfaces. Mussels are harvested mainly through March, April, May, and again in October and November.

Hot 'n' Sour Shrimp Soup

Ingredients

- 2 pounds raw shrimp
- 1 teaspoon sesame oil
- ¼ cup green onion, minced
- ½ cup red pepper, diced
- ½ cup yellow pepper, diced
- ½ cup jalapeño pepper, diced
- 2 cups spinach, julienned
- 1 cup chicken stock
- 2 cups seafood stock
- ½ cup pineapple juice
- ½ cup crushed pineapple
- ¼ cup lemon juice
- zest of 1 lemon
- zest of 1 lime
- 1 tablespoon fresh ginger root, grated
- 1 tablespoon soya sauce
- 1 tablespoon Worcestershire sauce
- ½ teaspoon dried dill
- ½ teaspoon dried basil
- salt and pepper to taste
- water to cover

Method

1. Clean and prepare shrimp as per instructions on page 40.

2. Place all ingredients except the shrimp and sesame oil in a large deep pot. Cover with water so the water level is 2 inches above ingredients.

3. Bring to a boil, reduce heat, and let simmer on low for 20 minutes. Add sesame oil and shrimp, cook until shrimp are pink and curled tightly, about 5 minutes.

4. Serve piping hot.

Hint: For added flair you may leave the shrimp with the shells on, for a more hands-on-style soup.

Serves 4

Scrumptious Shellfish Soup

Method

1. Place everything except seafood in a deep stock pot and bring to a rolling boil. Cook until onions are transparent, about 10 to 15 minutes.

2. Add all seafood and cook for an additional 20 minutes over medium heat.

3. Sprinkle with sesame seeds and serve piping hot.

Hint: You may need to add additional stock as the vegetables cook and the liquid evaporates. Keep the liquid over the seafood by at least 1 inch at all times.

Serves 6–10

Seaweed is high in potassium, calcium, and iron; it is also considered a natural detoxifier. Some say seaweed reduces the gaseous attributes in foods like beans and cabbage. Seaweed is defined by some as wet and fresh, while the sun-cured version is often referred to as dulse.

Ingredients

> 2 cups shrimp

> 1 cup lobster meat, chopped

> 1 cup baby scallops

> 2 cups raw mussels, shelled

> 1 cup crab meat, chopped

> 2 litres chicken stock

> ½ cup carrot, peeled and diced

> 1 cup red pepper, diced

> 1 cup plum tomatoes, chopped

> ½ cup red onion, minced

> ½ cup green onion, sliced

> 2 cloves garlic, minced

> 1 tablespoon fresh basil

> 1 tablespoon fresh parsley

> 1 teaspoon dried dill

> ½ cup lemon juice

> zest of 1 lemon

> 1 tablespoon sesame seeds

Coquilles St. Jacques Scallop Bisque

Ingredients

- 2 pounds scallops, uncooked
- 6 slices bacon
- ¼ cup clarified butter (recipe on page 2)
- 1 cup onion, minced
- 2 cloves garlic, minced
- 1 teaspoon fresh ginger root, grated
- ½ cup celery, minced
- 2 cups potatoes, peeled and diced
- 1 tablespoon lemon juice
- 1 cup heavy cream
- 1 cup evaporated milk
- 1 teaspoon dried dill
- ½ teaspoon nutmeg
- water or stock to cover
- salt and pepper to taste

Method

1. Clean scallops well, then set aside.

2. In a large frying pan, cook bacon. Remove strips from pan and reserve grease.

3. Add butter to the bacon grease and fry scallops until golden brown. Remove from heat and pat dry. Reserve 1 tablespoon of grease.

4. Place 1 ½ pounds of scallops in a bowl and set aside. Place the other ½ pound of scallops in a separate bowl and set aside.

5. Fry onion, garlic, and ginger in the same frying pan with the reserved bacon grease. Remove from heat and drain off any remaining bacon grease. Discard any remaining grease once cooled.

6. In a large stock pot, combine all ingredients except scallops.

7. Simmer over low to medium heat until potatoes start to fall apart, approximately 30 minutes.

Continued next page...

8. Add 1 and ½ pounds of scallops and cook for 5 additional minutes.

9. Purée soup with hand blender or food processor for 5 minutes. Be careful when blending hot liquids, as they cause containers to expand and lids to get stuck. Make sure the hot liquid is vented. You can always cool the soup first, purée it, and then reheat if you prefer.

10. Flash fry the reserved ½ pound of scallops until they are just warm. Chop them roughly and sprinkle over top of each bowl just before serving.

Note: Reduce the fat content by using a nonstick pan, and discarding the bacon fat in step 3. The cream and milk may also be substituted for a lower-fat options.

Serves 4–8

The Self-Contained Underwater Breathing Apparatus (SCUBA) tank was invented in New Brunswick by James Elliott and Alexander McAvity in 1839. This holding tank of air for divers made it very easy to gather scallops from the cold waters. Divers could stay under water longer, thus collecting more scallops, and making more money with their bigger catches.

Mom's Mussel and Barley Stew

Ingredients

- 3 pounds raw mussels, in the shell
- 1 cup small shell-shaped pasta, uncooked
- ½ cup pearl barley, uncooked
- ¼ cup bacon, cooked and crumbled
- 2 cups stewed tomatoes, chopped
- 1 cup onion, minced
- ½ cup leek, sliced
- 1 cup zucchini, diced
- 1 cup mushrooms, thinly sliced
- ½ cup carrots, peeled and minced
- 1 cup dry white wine
- 2 cups chicken broth
- 1 tablespoon dried basil
- ½ teaspoon dried oregano
- 1 teaspoon dried dill
- ½ teaspoon cumin
- salt and pepper to taste

Method

1. Clean and prepare mussels according to technique on page 40.

2. Place everything except mussels into a large stock pot.

3. Bring to a rolling boil, then reduce heat to low and simmer until barley is tender, about 30 to 45 minutes.

4. Add mussels, cover, and cook for 10 minutes, or until shells pop open.

Suggestion: Serve with bread for dipping or dumplings.

Serves 4–8

Sweet and Succulent Scallop Stew

Method

1. Cook bacon. Pat dry on paper towel, then crumble. Reserve grease.

2. In the leftover bacon grease, sauté ginger, garlic, onions, celery, and carrots over medium heat until tender.

3. Add everything except milk and scallops into a deep pot. Make sure liquid covers ingredients by about 3 inches.

4. Cook over medium heat until potatoes are tender. Add milk and scallops and simmer for 5 more minutes.

Serves 4–8

Ingredients

- 2 slices bacon

- ½ teaspoon fresh ginger root, grated

- 1 clove garlic, minced

- 1 cup onion, minced

- ½ cup celery, minced

- ½ cup carrots, minced

- 2 cups potatoes, peeled and diced small

- 1 tablespoon mustard

- 1 tablespoon Worcestershire sauce

- 1 tablespoon soya sauce

- 1 tablespoon sesame oil

- 4 cups chicken stock

- 1 teaspoon dill

- 2 pounds small scallops (or large ones, quartered)

- 1 cup evaporated milk

Lobster Bisque with Fiddleheads

Ingredients

> 1 pound lobster meat, diced

> 1 pound lobster knuckles and claws, in the shell

> 2 slices bacon, cooked and crumbled (grease reserved)

> 2 tablespoons clarified butter (recipe on page 2)

> 1 cup onion, minced

> 1 cup mushrooms, thinly sliced

> ½ cup celery, minced

> 2 cloves garlic, minced

> 2 cups potatoes, peeled and diced

> water or stock to cover

> 1 tablespoon soya sauce

Method

1. If using lobster in the shell, reserve shells to produce great stock. See Simple Seafood Broth recipe page 55.

2. In a large frying pan, melt reserved bacon grease and butter. Sauté onions, mushrooms, celery, and garlic until fragrant and golden.

3. Add potatoes, and fry for 2 minutes. Remove from heat and place all into a deep stock pot. Cover mixture with water or stock until liquid is 2 inches above ingredients.

4. Add soya sauce, Worcestershire sauce, dill, nutmeg, zest, salt, and pepper. Bring to a rolling boil over high heat until potatoes are half-cooked. Add fiddleheads and lobster. Reduce heat to medium and simmer until fiddleheads are tender, about 10 minutes.

5. Add cream and bacon bits, stir well, and cook for 5 minutes on low heat, stirring occasionally to ensure milk does not burn.

Continued next page...

Suggestion: This creamy soup is delicious with dumplings! To make the dumplings directly in the pot, add dough at the end of step 4 (recipe on page 141). Wait until dumplings are ¾ cooked, then add milk and increase heat to medium. Cover pot and steam about 5 additional minutes.

You could also serve with puff pastry cut with seafood-shaped cookie cutters instead of the more traditional bread sticks or biscuits, or try cutting biscuits into fun seafood shapes!

Serves 4–8

> 1 tablespoon Worcestershire sauce

> ½ teaspoon dried dill

> ½ teaspoon nutmeg

> 1 teaspoon lemon zest

> salt and pepper to taste

> 1 cup fiddleheads, rinsed and diced

> 2 cups heavy cream

From the Sea

Almost 50 percent of the world's lobster supply is harvested from Atlantic waters. The fishery is based on rotating regions to allow for natural replenishment of the stocks. Lobster fishers in New Brunswick pride themselves in maintaining a sustainable industry. It takes a lobster 4 to 7 years to reach market size. Lobsters molt as they grow, wiggling out of their hard shell so they can grow a new and bigger shell. Molting takes (on average) 5 to 20 minutes, then the lobster drinks large amounts of water for the next few hours to gain weight. After purchasing, lobsters are best stored between 33–40°C or 91–104°F. They live in salt water and must be alive when you cook them. Some folks say the cold deep waters of the North Atlantic adds a taste you can't quite describe or replace.

Creamy Mussel Chowder

Ingredients

- 3 pounds raw mussels, shelled with juice reserved

- 1 pound raw mussels in shell

- 2 cups potatoes, peeled and diced

- 1 tablespoon soya sauce

- 1 tablespoon Worcestershire sauce

- ½ cup onion, diced

- ½ cup celery, diced

- ½ cup carrots, peeled and diced

- ½ cup mushrooms, sliced

- 2 cups chicken stock

- 1 teaspoon dill

- ½ teaspoon oregano

- ¼ teaspoon nutmeg

- water to cover

- 1 cup heavy cream

Method

1. Clean and prepare mussels as per instructions on page 40.

2. In a deep pot, place potatoes, soya sauce, Worcestershire sauce, onion, celery, carrots, mushrooms, chicken stock, dill, oregano, and nutmeg.

3. Add enough cold water to cover the ingredients by 3 inches. Cover and simmer over low heat until potatoes are tender, about 15 minutes.

4. Add cream and all of the mussels.

5. Continue to cook until mussels in the shell open up, about 10 minutes.

Serves 4–8

Hearty Lobster Chowder

Method

1. Place all ingredients in a deep pot. Simmer over low heat for about 1 hour, stirring often.

Ingredients

> 2 pounds raw lobster meat, cleaned and chopped

> 1 pound lobster claws, cleaned and in the shell

> 1 cup dry white wine

> 2 cups evaporated milk

> 3 cups chicken or vegetable stock

> 1 cup sour cream* (optional)

> 2 cups potatoes, peeled and cubed

> ½ cup onion, minced

> ¾ cup red pepper, minced

> 1 cup celery, minced

> ¼ cup bacon, cooked and crumbled

> 1 clove garlic, minced

> 1 teaspoon dried rosemary

> 2 tablespoons dried parsley

> 1 teaspoon cumin

> 1 tablespoon butter*

> salt and pepper to taste

Fat-free option: Use skim milk or fat-free sour cream and omit the butter.

Sea kayaking is an increasingly popular aquatic adventure. St. George, St. Andrews, and Bathurst are great spots to visit and to arrange a tour to get up close and personal with the waters surrounding New Brunswick.

Fundy Fish Chowder

Ingredients

- 2 pounds white fish, cubed

- ½ pound salmon, cubed

- 1 cup baby clams, canned (with juice)

- 1 cup baby shrimp, canned or fresh

- ½ cup dry white wine

- 4 cups chicken stock

- 2 cups evaporated milk

- 2 cups potatoes, peeled and cubed

- ½ cup red pepper, minced

- ½ cup mushroom, minced

- 1 cup celery, minced

- ½ cup onion, minced

- ½ cup carrots, peeled and diced

- ⅛ cup bacon, cooked and crumbled

- 2 cloves garlic, minced

- 1 teaspoon dried rosemary

- ½ teaspoon dried dill

Method

1. Place all ingredients in a deep pot. Simmer over low heat for about 1 hour, stirring often.

2. Serve with a Maritime Lobster Croissant (recipe on page 105), for a soup-and-sandwich combo that is pure New Brunswick.

Kouchibouguac National Park offers the warmest salt water north of Virginia. Swimming, nature hikes, biking trails, and excellent camping facilities await.

Maritime Clam Chowder

Method

1. Melt butter and sauté onion until soft.

2. Place all of the ingredients into a large pot and simmer on low until potatoes are tender. About 1 hour.

3. Serve piping hot with crusty bread or tea biscuits.

Ingredients

- 1 tablespoon butter

- ½ cup onion, diced

- 3 cups fresh baby clams, cleaned and uncooked (or canned clams, including juice)

- 1 cup mushroom, sliced

- 2 cups potatoes, diced

- ½ cup green tomato, diced

- ¼ cup bacon, crispy and finely chopped

- 1 cup heavy cream

- 1 cup condensed cream of chicken soup (or skim milk)

- 2 cups evaporated milk

- 5 cups chicken or vegetable stock

- 1 tablespoon dried parsley

- 1 teaspoon dried rosemary

- 1 teaspoon chili powder

- ½ teaspoon dried dill

Lighthouse Spicy Seafood Boil

Ingredients

- 1 pound small mussels in the shell
- 1 pound baby clams
- 1 pound lobster meat
- 1 pound lobster claws in the shell
- 1 pound baby scallops
- 1 pound shrimp
- 1 cup onion, diced
- 1 cup mushroom, sliced
- 1 cup celery, diced
- ¼ cup jalapeño pepper minced
- 2 cloves garlic, minced
- 2 cups tomato juice
- 2 cups stewed tomatoes, chopped
- 4 cups chicken stock
- 1 teaspoon cumin
- 1 tablespoon dried basil
- 1 teaspoon dried oregano
- 1 teaspoon cayenne pepper
- 1 teaspoon chili pepper
- salt and pepper to taste

Method

1. Clean all seafood and set aside.

2. Place all ingredients into a large deep pot. Stir gently and cover. Let simmer on low for 1 hour, stirring occasionally.

3. Serve piping hot with garlic bread or baguette.

Serves 8–12

Commercial fishing is the fourth-largest industry in New Brunswick after forestry, mining, and agriculture. Lobster, crab, and salmon are the largest crops in fishing.

Simple Seafood Broth

This is a way to get the most flavour out of any seafood dish you make. When you use seafood for a specific recipe, save the shells or bones to make some very flavourful broth. This can be made with any type of shellfish: mussels, clams, lobster, shrimp, etc., and for fish, the bones and skin carry the flavour.

Method

1. Preheat oven to 450°.

2. Spread shells, skins, and/or bones on a cookie sheet and roast them until they start to blacken, between 15 to 30 minutes. Remove from oven.

3. Add all ingredients to a deep pot and cover with water. Bring to a rolling boil, then reduce heat to low and simmer for 1 hour.

4. Strain all items out (including peppercorns, vegetables, shells, and bones) and use broth in soups, chowders, casseroles, sauces, or dips.

Ingredients

> 2 pounds (or more) seafood shells or bones, all meat removed

> 2 tablespoons whole black peppercorns

> 1 lemon, cut in half

> 3 stalks celery

> 2 whole carrots, unpeeled

> 1 medium-sized onion, unpeeled

> 2 medium-sized potatoes, unpeeled

> 1 (3 to 6 inch) piece seaweed, if available

> 1 beach rock freshly picked and scrubbed with soap and water (optional)

> water to cover, about 4 to 12 litres

Lobster and Spinach Stuffed Mushrooms

Ingredients

> 1 pound lobster meat

> mushrooms*

> 1 pound baby spinach, rinsed and chopped

> 1 cup cream cheese

> 1 teaspoon dried dill

> 1 teaspoon lemon zest

> 1 clove garlic

> salt and pepper to taste

Mushrooms: Use 12 large stuffing mushrooms which can be found at most local grocery stores. If using button baby mushrooms, you will need at least 2 pounds If using the portobello variety use 6.

Method

1. Preheat oven to 450°.

2. Clean and prepare mushrooms by removing their stems so you can stuff the caps.

3. Place all ingredients except lobster into a blender or food processor and purée until smooth.

4. Add lobster and pulse or blend slowly so lobster remains a little chunky.

5. Stuff mushroom caps and place them on a lined cookie sheet or in a shallow casserole dish.

6. Bake or broil until cheese is golden brown, about 10 to 20 minutes. Try cooking these mushrooms on the barbecue for a smokier flavour!

Hint: You can incorporate the mushroom stems into the stuffing by adding them to the food processor in step 3, or save them for another meal or the stock pot.

Serves 4–10

Oysters Rockefeller

Method

1. Preheat oven to 500°

2. Clean oysters and spread them onto a cookie sheet. Open them flat so they lie on the half shell. Set the cookie sheet aside.

3. In a bowl, mix all of the ingredients (except the Parmesan cheese) until well blended. Spoon 1 to 2 tablespoons on top of each oyster.

4. Sprinkle each oyster with Parmesan cheese and broil until cheese is browned, about 3 to 5 minutes.

Serves 2–4 (6 per person as an hors-d'oeuvre or 18 per person as a main course)

Ingredients

- 2 pounds fresh oysters

- ¼ cup bacon, crispy and finely chopped

- 2 cups spinach, cleaned and chopped

- ¼ cup onion, minced

- ½ cup very fine bread crumbs

- ¼ cup hot sauce

- ½ cup oyster juice

- 1 tablespoon anise-flavoured liqueur (Anisette or Sambuca)

- ½ cup Parmesan cheese, freshly grated

From the Sea

Did you know? Malpeque oysters are one of New Brunswick's famous local treasures.

Raspberry Oysters Rockefeller

Serve these oysters with a nice side salad or over a bed of rice.
Toss in some crusty bread to soak up all those tasty juices.

Ingredients

- 4 pounds raw oysters

- 1 cup fresh raspberries*

- ½ cup apple juice

- 1 tablespoon soya sauce

- 1 tablespoon Worcestershire sauce

- ¼ cup fresh fennel, grated

- ½ teaspoon dried dill

- ¼ cup lemon juice

- 1 tablespoon lemon zest

- 1 tablespoon butter

- ½ cup onion, minced

- ½ cup celery, minced

- 1 teaspoon licorice-flavoured liqueur (Pernod, Anisette, or Ouzo)

- salt and pepper to taste

Method

1. Preheat oven to 450°.

2. Clean oysters well. Open shells, making sure to retain the juices. Lay oysters as flat as possible in a shallow 9 x 13 baking dish. Set aside.

3. In a medium mixing bowl, place the raspberries, apple juice, soya sauce, Worcestershire sauce, fennel, dill, lemon juice, and zest. Stir until even, then set aside.

4. In a large frying pan, melt the butter and sauté the onion and celery until tender.

5. Add fruit mixture to the frying pan and stir. Bring mixture to a rolling boil for 3 minutes. Remove from heat, add liqueur, and stir.

6. Spoon 1 tablespoon over each oyster. Any leftover sauce can be reserved for dipping.

7. Broil for 15 minutes, or until topping starts to bubble and roast.

Serves 4–8

Try strawberries, blueberries, blackberries, or even diced apple!

APPETIZERS, SAUCES, & DIPS

Oyster beds are found along river mouths and inlets on the southern Gulf of St. Lawrence and the Northumberland Strait all the way to Cape Breton. The two halves of the shell are equal in size but the top one is flat while the bottom one is curved to house the oyster. The shell is rough and sculptured in appearance, and the colour varies from brown, grey, green, to white.

The inside of the shell is superbly smooth with a dull white finish. Spring and fall are the two seasons for harvest, and oysters typically range in size from 3 to 10 inches in diameter.

An oyster can take up to seven years to reach market size. They have slightly salty but plump flesh. The shape and size determines the quality or grade. They are harvested with hand-held rakes. Oysters require water to breathe and should be kept in their own juice around 5°C/40°F. Oyster juice is a prized item and you can find it bottled in any grocery store. When shucking oysters, reserve as much juice as you can for your dish. During oyster season you may find oyster shucking contests at local festivals.

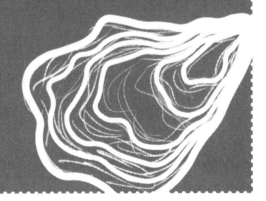

Crab Caesar Salad

Ingredients

- ½ cup Caesar salad dressing (recipe on page 118)

- 1 tablespoon Worcestershire sauce

- 1 teaspoon lemon juice

- ¼ cup Parmesan cheese, grated

- 1 teaspoon dried dill

- salt and pepper to taste

- 2 pounds crab meat, cooked and chopped

- 1 head of romaine lettuce, rinsed and chopped

- 1 cup of croutons (recipe on page 146)

- 3 strips bacon, cooked and crumbled

- lemon wedges to garnish

Method

1. In a large salad bowl, mix the Caesar dressing, Worcestershire sauce, lemon juice, Parmesan cheese, dill, salt, and pepper together until even.

2. Add crab, toss well to coat. Add lettuce, croutons, and bacon bits.

1. Toss and serve immediately. Garnish with lemon wedges.

Hint: This recipe can be made with many variations of shellfish or seafood.

By the Shore Shrimp Caesar: add 2 pounds baby shrimp.

Atlantic Lobster Caesar: add 2 pounds lobster meat (knuckles, claws, tail).

Zesty Salmon Caesar: add 2 pounds cooked salmon chunks.

Drunken Side of Salmon

Method

1. Preheat oven to 400°.

2. Clean salmon well. Place fillets into a casserole dish and set aside.

3. In a small bowl, mix soya sauce, Worcestershire sauce, chicken stock, lime juice, zests, sugar, and tequila into a bowl and mix well.

4. Pour mixture over fish and season with salt and pepper.

5. Top with slices of lime, cover, and bake for 25 minutes.

6. Serve with rice and vegetables or a side salad.

Serves 4–6

Hint: Alcohol, when used in cooking, leaves the flavour of the spirit without the effects of the alcohol, which evaporates when heated. There may be some residual alcohol, so be aware of this when serving others, especially pregnant women or children.

Ingredients

- 2 pounds salmon fillets

- 1 tablespoon soya sauce

- 1 tablespoon Worcestershire sauce

- 1 cup chicken stock

- 1 cup lime juice

- zest of 1 lemon

- zest of 1 lime

- 1 tablespoon white sugar

- ¼ cup tequila

- 2 whole limes, sliced

- salt and pepper to taste

From the Sea

Sweet Summer Salmon Salsa

Ingredients

- 1 (15-ounce) can mandarin oranges, drained and loosely chopped, juice reserved

- 1 tablespoon soya sauce

- 1 tablespoon Worcestershire sauce

- 1 pound of salmon cleaned, cooked, and broken into bite-sized chunks

- 1 firm avocado, diced small

- ½ cup red onion, minced

- 1 tablespoon dried dill

- 1 teaspoon cayenne pepper

- salt and pepper to taste

Method

1. In a small bowl, whisk juice from mandarin oranges, soya sauce, and Worcestershire sauce and set aside.

2. In a separate, bigger bowl, mix everything else until combined.

3. Pour sauce over salad and toss until evenly coated.

Suggestion: Serve cold on a large leaf of lettuce, or toss with cold pasta. You could also use as a dip for vegetables or chips, or heat it and serve over pasta.

Makes approximately 3 cups

Periwinkles

Serve these little delicacies as an appetizer or as a
main dish with a side salad and crusty bread.

Method

1. Preheat oven to 400°.

2. Clean periwinkles and place in an escargot bowl or
    any shallow baking dish.

3. Cover with alfredo sauce and bake uncovered for
    20 minutes.

4. Remove from oven, sprinkle Parmesan and then
    mozzarella cheese. Return to oven and broil until
    cheese is bubbly and melted, about 5 to 10 minutes.

Ingredients

> 2 pounds fresh periwinkles

> alfredo sauce (recipe on
  page 116), cooled

> ½ cup Parmesan cheese,
  shredded

> 1 cup mozzarella cheese,
  shredded

Hot 'n' Spicy Seafood Rub

This tasty seasoning is delicious on any type of seafood (and chicken) but is especially good on shrimp, cod, or salmon.

Ingredients

- 2 tablespoons cumin

- 2 tablespoons curry powder

- 2 tablespoons black pepper

- 2 tablespoons coriander powder

- 1 tablespoon garlic powder

- 2 teaspoons cayenne pepper

- 1 teaspoon dried basil

- 1 teaspoon crushed chilies

- 1 teaspoon salt

Method

1. Stir everything in a small bowl until evenly mixed.

2. Sprinkle over seafood, rubbing in gently so each piece is coated well.

3. Cook on barbecue or broil in the oven until seafood is fully cooked.

Makes approximately ¾ cup

Lemon-Dill Butter

Method

1. In a deep medium-sized bowl, cream all ingredients until seasonings are evenly incorporated.

Suggestion: Use this tangy spread anywhere you would use butter. Will keep in fridge for up to 2 weeks.

Makes approximately 2 cups

Ingredients

> 1 pound butter, at room temperature

> zest of 1 lemon

> 1 tablespoon dried dill

> black pepper to taste

Anchovy Garlic Butter

Ingredients

> 1 pound butter, room temperature

> 1 tablespoon roasted garlic mashed (or 1 teaspoon, freshly minced)

> ¼ cup anchovies, minced

> 1 tablespoon lemon zest

Method

1. Cream all ingredients in a small bowl until incorporated.

Suggestion: Use over any type of seafood any time a recipe calls for butter. Store in fridge for up to 2 weeks.

Hot Shrimp Dip

This dish is great whenever a group gathers. Delicious when made with shrimp, it also works well with salmon, tuna, crab, scallops, lobster, or even chicken!

Method

1. Preheat oven to 350°.

2. Purée all ingredients in a food processor or blender until smooth.

3. Spread in a shallow casserole dish and bake for 15 minutes until bubbly.

Suggestion: Serve with crusty bread, nacho chips, or pita for dipping. Alternatively, store in an airtight container and refrigerate for 2 hours before serving chilled with vegetables or crackers.

Makes approximately 3 cups

Ingredients

> 1 cup herbed or plain cream cheese, softened

> ¼ cup sour cream

> 2 cups cooked or canned shrimp

> 1 tablespoon green onion, minced

> 1 teaspoon jalapeño pepper, seeded and minced

> 1 clove garlic, minced

> 1 tablespoon lemon juice

> 1 teaspoon cayenne pepper

> ½ teaspoon paprika

> 1 tablespoon soya sauce

> 1 tablespoon Worcestershire sauce

> salt and pepper to taste

Salmon Dip

Ingredients

> 1 pound salmon, cooked and cooled

> 1 cup herbed or plain cream cheese

> ½ bag baby spinach, rinsed and chopped

> 1 tablespoon onion, minced

> 2 tablespoons red onion, minced

> 1 teaspoon lemon juice

> 1 teaspoon soya sauce

> ½ teaspoon dill dried

> ½ teaspoon cayenne pepper

> salt and pepper to taste

Method

1. Purée all of the ingredients in a blender or food processor until smooth.

2. Place in a serving dish. Cover and chill for 2 hours before serving with vegetables or crackers.

Makes approximately 2 cups

Authentic Seafood Pasta Sauce

Method

1. Place all ingredients into a large deep pot and simmer for 2 hours on low.

2. Serve over a bed of pasta (spaghetti, linguine, or angel hair work best, but use whatever type of pasta you prefer).

3. Top with grated Parmesan or Romano cheese.

Clams are usually found near the mouth of rivers and inlets and near some beaches. They live in the sand and mud around mid-tide level. They usually come in an oval-shaped shell which is thin and brittle and chalky white. Clams cannot close their shells entirely due to their long necks, which extend beyond the edge of their shells.

Ingredients

> ½ pound fresh raw mussels (in the shell)

> ½ pound fresh raw clams (in the shell)

> 2 cups canned baby clams with juice

> 1 cup fresh shrimp

> 2 cups mushrooms, sliced

> ½ cup onion, minced

> ½ cup celery, minced

> 1 cup zucchini, diced

> 2 cloves garlic, minced

> 1 cup beef stock

> 2 cups crushed tomatoes

> 1 cup condensed tomato soup

> 1 cup tomato paste

> 1 teaspoon dried oregano

> 1 teaspoon dried parsley

> 1 teaspoon dried basil

> ½ teaspoon dried mint

Fundy Shore Tartar Sauce

Ingredients

- 1 ½ cups mayonnaise*

- 1 cup green relish (or baby gherkin pickles, minced)

- ¼ cup onion, minced

- 1 clove garlic, minced

- ¼ cup lemon juice

- ¼ cup cider vinegar

- 1 teaspoon olive oil

- 1 teaspoon prepared mustard

- ½ teaspoon dried dill

- ¼ teaspoon paprika

- 1 teaspoon anchovy paste (optional)

- 1 teaspoon capers minced (optional)

Fat-free option: use cottage cheese, plain Greek yogurt, or fat-free sour cream instead of mayonnaise.

Method

1. Mix all ingredients in a deep bowl until smooth and creamy.

2. Let sit in refrigerator for 1 hour to allow the flavours to blend.

Suggestion: Serve as a condiment with any fish, French fries, or use as a sandwich spread.

Makes approximately 3 cups

Creamy Summer Shrimp Alfredo

This recipe is for an individual serving.

Method

1. Melt butter in a large pot and add garlic, red pepper, and onions. Add shrimp and sauté over medium heat until shrimp are pink and tender, about 5 minutes.

2. Add the pasta, milk, cream, parsley, salt, pepper, and hot peppers (if using). Toss until everything is evenly coated.

3. Bring liquid to a rolling boil and add the cheese. Stir constantly until thickened, about 4 minutes.

4. Turn off heat. Let sit 2 minutes before serving.

Hint: You can use skim milk and fat reduced cheese but this is a rich dish and a thick liquid like whipping cream is needed. You can use buttermilk which has less fat but it will alter the taste a little. If you make it fat free the mixture will be of a thinner consistency.

Ingredients

> 1 tablespoon butter

> ½ clove garlic, minced

> ¼ cup red pepper, diced

> 1 teaspoon onion, minced

> ½ pound raw shrimp

> 1 cup cooked pasta*

> ½ cup milk

> ½ cup heavy cream

> ½ teaspoon dried parsley

> dash of salt

> ½ teaspoon white pepper

> 1 tablespoon hot chili peppers (optional)

> ¼ cup Parmesan cheese, grated

*Use whatever pasta you prefer, such as linguine, penne, fusilli, or bowtie.

PASTA

71

Mediterranean Mussel Pasta

Ingredients

- 2 pounds raw mussels, in the shell

- 1 tablespoon olive oil

- 1 cup sweet onion, diced

- 1 cup mushrooms, sliced

- 2 cups stewed tomatoes, chopped with juice

- 1 cup zucchini, sliced

- ½ cup black olives, pitted and sliced

- ½ cup green olives, pitted and sliced

- 1 tablespoon soya sauce

- 1 tablespoon Worcestershire sauce

- 1 cup chicken stock

- ½ cup apple juice

- 450g pasta (spaghetti, angel hair, linguine, or fettuccini), cooked

- Parmesan or feta cheese for garnish (optional)

Method

1. Clean and prepare mussels as per instructions on page 40.

2. In a large frying pan, heat oil and sauté onion for 1 minute. Add mushrooms and tomatoes, and cook for 2 additional minutes over high heat.

3. Lower heat to medium and add zucchini, olives, soya sauce, Worcestershire sauce, chicken stock, and apple juice. Simmer for 10 minutes.

4. Add mussels, lower heat to low, cover the pan tightly with a lid, and simmer until mussel shells open, about 10 to 15 minutes. Discard any mussels that do not open.

5. Pour sauce over freshly cooked hot pasta. Sprinkle with grated Parmesan or crumbled feta cheese.

Serves 4–6

Serve mussels tonight! Did you know mussels are low in fat and carbohydrates? They are also a great source of protein, vitamins, and minerals.

Succulent Seafood Lasagna

Method

1. In a large stock pot, heat the oil and sauté mushrooms and onion until golden.

2. Add seafood, tomato sauce, stock, cocktail sauce, soya sauce, Worcestershire sauce, basil, dill, nutmeg, salt, and pepper and bring everything to a slow simmer. Let sauce simmer on lowest heat until it reduces by one third, about 30 to 45 minutes.

3. Meanwhile, in a deep bowl, mix cottage and mozzarella cheeses and set aside.

4. Preheat oven to 350°. In a 9 x 13 dish, spread a thin layer of tomato sauce over the bottom.

5. Place 4 noodles across the pan, then spread half the cheese mixture over top of the noodles. Layer sauce on top of the cheese, followed by noodles, followed by cheese. Repeat until all ingredients are used.

6. Bake uncovered for 30 to 45 minutes, or until sauce bubbles.

Serves 4–8

Ingredients

- 1 tablespoon olive oil
- 1 cup mushrooms, sliced
- ½ cup onion, minced
- 3 cups seafood (such as cod, haddock, shrimp, scallops, mussels, salmon, etc.)
- 4 cups tomato sauce
- 1 cup stock (fish, beef, chicken, or vegetable)
- 1 cup seafood cocktail sauce
- 1 tablespoon soya sauce
- 1 tablespoon Worcestershire sauce
- 1 tablespoon dried basil
- dash dried dill
- dash nutmeg
- salt and pepper to taste
- 2 cups cottage cheese
- 2 cups mozzarella cheese, shredded
- 16 strips lasagna noodles, cooked and cooled

Did you know? Lobsters prefer deep dark places and are most active at night, which makes them hard for scientists to study. Did you know a lobster has two bladders and they both are located in the head?

From the Bay of Chaleur to the Bay of Fundy, the waters of New Brunswick offer locals and visitors alike some of the finest and freshest seafood around. There is an abundance of succulent seafood throughout the coastal communities, so make sure to partake in this incredible coastal culinary experience.

Visit Campbellton during summertime for their annual Salmon Festival. This festival originated in Canada's centennial year, 1967. The warmer months are filled with festivals celebrating the many diverse cultures that helped establish our beautiful province.

Linguine Alfredo with Mussels

Method

1. Clean and prepare mussels, see page 40.

2. Place all ingredients except cheese and spinach in a thick-bottomed saucepan and bring to a boil. Add the cheese, stirring constantly until sauce is slightly thickened.

3. Remove from heat and serve over julienned spinach.

4. Serve with toasted garlic bread.

Serves 2–4

Ingredients

- 1 pound mussels per person, in shell

- 450g cooked linguine noodles, spinach variety

- 1 teaspoon garlic butter

- ½ cup heavy cream

- ½ cup milk

- 1 tablespoon soya sauce

- 1 tablespoon Worcestershire sauce

- ½ teaspoon lemon zest

- dash of dried dill

- salt and pepper to taste

- ½ cup Parmesan cheese, shredded

- 1 cup baby spinach per person, rinsed and julienned

Bay Scallops with Linguine, Dill and Mushrooms

This recipe is for an individual serving.

Ingredients

- 1 tablespoon butter

- ½ clove garlic, minced

- ½ teaspoon dried dill

- 1 tablespoon red onion, minced

- 1 cup mushrooms, sliced

- salt and pepper to taste

- ½ pound scallops, cleaned and sliced

- ¾ cup cooked linguine

- 1 cup spinach, rinsed and julienned

- Parmesan cheese to garnish

- 1 teaspoon fresh parsley, chopped

Method

1. Melt butter in a large frying pan and add garlic, dill, onion, mushrooms, salt, and pepper. Toss in scallops and sauté over medium heat until cooked, about 5 minutes.

2. Add pasta and toss until warmed through.

3. Add spinach and toss until leaves are wilted.

4. Serve hot and garnish with parsley and freshly grated Parmesan cheese.

Blueberry Cod on Citrus Rice

Method

1. Preheat oven to 400°. Clean fish, place in a 9 x 13 casserole dish, cover, and set aside in fridge.

2. Mix all of the remaining ingredients in a saucepan and bring to a boil.

3. Remove from heat and mash berries. Strain mixture, reserving ½ cup for the rice recipe, and pour the rest over the fish. Bake uncovered for 25 minutes.

4. Meanwhile, prepare the rice according to package instructions substituting ½ cup of the liquid required with the reserved blueberry mixture.

5. Fluff with a fork, lay fish on top, and serve with fresh berries or lemon slices.

Serves 4–6

Blueberry Cod

- 2 pounds fresh cod fillets

- 2 cups large blueberries, rinsed

- 1 cup apple juice

- 1 cup chicken broth

- 1 cup lemon juice

- ½ cup lime juice

- ¼ cup white sugar

- ¼ cup fresh parsley, chopped

- ¼ teaspoon nutmeg

Citrus Rice

- 2 cups rice, uncooked

- ½ cup reserved blueberry mixture

- fresh blueberries or lemon slices for garnish

MAINS

Leek and Salmon Pizza

Ingredients

> 1 (12-inch) pizza crust

> 1 tablespoon olive oil

> 1 cup soft cheese (cottage, goat, or cream cheese) at room temperature

> 1 teaspoon dill dried

> 1 teaspoon cumin

> 1 teaspoon dried basil

> salt and pepper to taste

> 1 pound smoked salmon, thinly sliced or flaked apart

> 1 cup plum tomatoes, diced

> 1 cup leeks*, thinly sliced

> ½ cup mozzarella cheese, grated

> ¼ cup sesame oil

> 1 tablespoon sesame seeds

Method

1. Preheat oven to 375°.

2. Drizzle olive oil on a pizza pan and spread out dough.

3. Spread cheese evenly over pizza dough. (Soften the cheese by microwaving if necessary.)

4. Sprinkle dill, cumin, basil, salt, and pepper over the cheese. Add salmon, then layer on tomatoes, and leeks, and top with mozzarella cheese.

5. Brush the edge of the crust with sesame oil and dust with seeds. Drizzle any left over sesame oil over top of cheese.

6. Bake until cheese is golden and bubbly, about 15 to 20 minutes.

Serves 4–6

*Cleaning a leek is easy: slice it from top to bottom to just about 1 inch above the root, rotate, and cut again to make an X. This will allow you to fan it out under running water to rinse off any dirt stuck under the leek's layered leaves.

Lobster with Creamed Peas

Try serving this as a main course over rice, noodles, or in a pie shell. It also works well as a side dish, and can be served hot or at room temperature.

Method

1. Cook peas in salted boiling water until tender, approximately 5 to 10 minutes. Drain.

2. Stir all remaining ingredients in a deep pot until all is coated and evenly mixed. Cook over medium heat until lobster is hot, about 10 minutes.

Serves 4–6

Ingredients

- 2 pounds sweet garden peas, cleaned and shelled
- 2 pounds lobster meat, chopped (raw or cooked), juice in
- ½ cup onion, minced
- 1 teaspoon Worcestershire sauce
- 1 teaspoon soya sauce
- ¼ cup lemon juice
- zest of 1 lemon
- ½ cup sour cream
- 1 teaspoon dried dill
- salt and pepper to taste

Maple Mussel Cream Pie

Ingredients

- 2 Savoury Pie Crust (recipe on page 177)

- 2 tablespoons clarified butter (recipe on page 2)

- 1 cup onion, minced

- 1 cup mushrooms, sliced

- 2 pounds raw mussels, shelled and juice in

- ½ cup maple syrup

- ¼ cup heavy cream

- salt and pepper to taste

- dash dried dill

- dash nutmeg

- 1 teaspoon cornstarch

- ½ cup mozzarella cheese, shredded

- 2 cups whipped* potatoes, cooked and cooled

Whipped potatoes are simply regular mashed potatoes with extra cream and/ or butter. Beat them with a hand mixer so they are extra fluffy and creamy.

Method

1. Preheat oven to 425°.

2. Clean and prepare mussels as per instructions on page 40.

3. Grease a pie plate and place one crust in the bottom. Set aside.

4. In a small frying pan, melt butter and sauté the onion and mushrooms until tender. Set aside.

5. In a deep bowl, mix mussels with sautéed vegetables, add maple syrup, cream, salt, pepper, dill, and nutmeg. Stir to incorporate.

6. Pour mixture into the pie shell. Sprinkle with cornstarch, then cover with mozzarella. Spread potatoes on top of cheese.

7. Gently place top crust, squeezing together edges. Use a fork to poke vent holes in top layer.

8. Bake for 20 to 25 minutes, or until crust is golden and juice begins to bubble.

Serves 6–8

Greek Shrimp with Lemon-Mint Cream Sauce

Method

1. In a large frying pan, melt butter with sesame oil over medium heat. Sauté the garlic, onion, jalapeño, celery, and ginger for about 2 minutes until fragrant.

2. Add shrimp and fry for 5 to 10 minutes, until the shrimp are pink and tightly curled.

3. Meanwhile, in a small bowl, mix the sour cream, lemon juice, and icing sugar until smooth. Add the zest, mint, hot pepper flakes, nutmeg, dill, salt, and pepper. Stir.

4. Pour the creamy mixture onto the shrimp, and cook until heated through, about 5 minutes.

5. Serve warm over a bed of rice.

Hint: If you prefer, you can leave the shells on the shrimp for a more hands-on meal, slurping the meat out of the shell!

Serves 3–6

Ingredients

- 1 tablespoon butter
- 1 tablespoon sesame oil
- 2 cloves garlic, minced
- ¼ cup onion, minced
- 1 teaspoon jalapeño pepper, diced
- ¼ cup celery, minced
- 1 teaspoon ginger root, grated
- 2 pounds raw shrimp, shells removed
- ½ cup sour cream
- 2 tablespoons lemon juice
- ¼ cup icing sugar, sifted
- 1 teaspoon lemon zest
- 1 tablespoon fresh mint, minced
- 1 teaspoon hot pepper flakes
- ¼ teaspoon nutmeg
- ¼ teaspoon dried dill
- salt and pepper to taste

Creamy Seafood Casserole

This dish can be made with any type of seafood like crab, cod, salmon, scallops, shrimp, haddock, or a combination. The recipe is a base, and I have listed the variations for each type of seafood (such as a cheese or vegetable that will enhance its flavour).

Ingredients

- 3 pounds seafood* of choice

- 1 tablespoon clarified butter (recipe on page 2)

- ½ cup onion, finely minced

- ½ cup celery, finely minced

- 2 cloves garlic, minced

- ¼ cup lemon juice

- 1 teaspoon dried dill

- salt and pepper to taste

- 1 teaspoon soya sauce

- 1 tablespoon Worcestershire sauce

- ½ cup heavy cream

- 1 recipe béchamel sauce (recipe on page 113), cooled

- 2 pounds mashed potatoes, cooled

Method

1. Clean seafood and pat dry. Preheat oven to 350°.

2. In a large frying pan, melt butter and sauté the seafood for 2 minutes per side, gaining some caramelization and flavour. (This is not to fully cook the seafood, just to add some colour and enhance the flavour.) Remove from heat and spread seafood evenly in the bottom of a 9 x 13 casserole dish.

3. In the same pan, sauté the onion, celery, and garlic until slightly golden. Remove from heat and add the lemon juice, dill, salt, pepper, soya sauce, and Worcestershire sauce. Pour this mixture evenly over the seafood.

4. Sprinkle evenly with cheese*. Spread a thin layer of mashed potato over top of the seafood and cheese, leaving a 1-inch gap from the outside edge of the dish on all sides.

Continued next page...

5. Pour béchamel sauce over top, ensuring it runs down through the one-inch border you left around the edge.

6. Bake uncovered for about 30 to 45 minutes, or until sauce bubbles in middle of pan and top becomes golden brown.

Hint: You may need to add a little water or stock to the casserole base in step 3 before adding the potatoes in step 4. Thin to desired consistency, and keep in mind the dish will thicken during cooking (and again as it cools).

Serves 6–10

Cod is a type of fish enjoyed by a variety of cultures. It is available commercially in a variety of forms from dried, salt cured, fresh, and pickled, to flakes, powder, oil, and tablets. It is used in recipes from breakfast to supper to dessert. Cod is a very versatile and delicious fish.

Commercial fishing has long been the sturdy backbone for many New Brunswick communities. Many people are employed in this industry which spans from the Gulf of Saint Lawrence to the Bay of Fundy. The main catch for most fishers is the great Atlantic lobster. Crab and herring are close behind. Salmon is the largest domestic farming resource we have for the fishing industry. Mussels and oysters from the Gulf of Saint Lawrence claim their fame in the cold waters there.

*Variations: *Use any one of the following, or a combination:*

White fish like cod, haddock, or sole: *Cut fish into 2-inch cubes. Use 1 cup of sharp cheddar, grated.*

Shrimp: *Clean, de-vein, and butterfly shrimp, making sure to remove all shells. Use ½ cup Parmesan, grated.*

Scallops: *Use baby ones or cut up the larger variety. Use ½ cup Parmesan and ¼ cup mild cheddar, grated.*

Crab or lobster: *Remove meat from shells. Use ¼ cup Parmesan, grated.*

Clams, mussels, or oysters: *Remove meat from shells (reserving any liquid for your dish). Use ¼ cup Parmesan grated, and add 1 teaspoon licorice-flavoured liqueur or extract.*

From the Sea

Salmon and Scallop Tartare

Ingredients

- ½ pound boneless salmon fillets, minced

- ½ pound baby scallops, minced

- ¼ teaspoon dill

- ½ teaspoon lemon juice

- salt and pepper to taste

- 1 tablespoon licorice-flavoured liqueur such as Pernod, Anisette, or Sambuca (optional)

Method

1. In a large bowl, combine the minced salmon and scallops.

2. Sprinkle with dill, lemon juice, salt, pepper, and liqueur (if using).

3. Shape into small cakes and serve raw on crispy toast rounds or crackers with a dollop of sour cream.

Hint: Be sure to only use the freshest seafood for this recipe and consume immediately; tartare does not make good leftovers!

Serves 2–6

Fish oil is a supplement known for its high content of vitamins A and D. It was recognized and invented in the daily dose form in 1921 by Hartley Wentworth from Deer Island. The popularity of fish oil's health benefits grew so large and quickly that the famous Ganong Bros. Limited chocolate company toyed with the idea of adding it to their chocolates to make it appealing to children.

Hot Thai Shrimp

Method

1. Bring all ingredients to a boil in a thick-bottomed sauce pot, until shrimp are pink and curled tight.

Suggestion: Serve with lots of crusty bread for dipping and soaking up that creamy sauce. Or, try dunking these shrimp in Peanut Sauce (recipe on page 122) for an authentic Thai flavour.

Serves 4–6

Ingredients

- 2 pounds shrimp, cleaned and in the shell
- ½ cup jalapeño pepper, chopped
- 1 teaspoon fresh ginger root, grated
- 1 clove garlic, minced
- 1 cup coconut milk
- 1 teaspoon soya sauce
- 1 teaspoon Worcestershire sauce
- 1 teaspoon dried dill

From the Sea

Thai food shouts of hotness and nutty flavours. Pairing barbecue nuts with ginger and garlic is a great culinary experience. Coconut is another familiar Thai ingredient.

Blackened Salmon

Ingredients

- 2 pounds fresh salmon

- 2 tablespoons cumin

- 2 tablespoons coriander

- 1 teaspoon salt

- 1 tablespoon black pepper

- 1 teaspoon crushed chilies

- zest of 1 lemon

- ¼ cup olive oil

- 1 whole lemon, cut into wedges

Method

1. Mix cumin, coriander, salt, pepper, chilies, and zest in food processor or blender until it is like dust.

2. Place salmon whole or cut up onto a cookie sheet lined with parchment paper. Brush with oil.

3. Sprinkle each piece with the spice mixture until well coated.

4. Broil in the oven or grill on the barbecue until salmon is blackened, approximately 10 to 25 minutes. Do not turn fish over.

5. Remove from heat and let sit for 5 minutes. Squeeze lemon juice over top and serve.

Serves 4

Tequila–Lime Barbecued Salmon

This dish is a perfect for summertime get-togethers!
Serve with potato salad or over a bed of rice.

Method

1. Preheat grill to medium.

2. Clean fish and place on a cookie sheet, skin-side down. Cover and set aside in fridge.

3. In a small bowl, mix the lime juice, zest, tequila, pepper, soya sauce, Worcestershire sauce, cilantro, brown sugar, and salt. Stir until the sugar is dissolved.

4. Brush the salmon pieces with this mixture, coating them generously.

5. Let sit for 5 minutes.

6. Grill on top rack in barbecue, skin-side down, until fully cooked, approximately 10 to 15 minutes. If there is any sauce left over, use it to baste during cooking.

Serves 4

Ingredients

> 4 salmon fillets or steaks

> ½ cup lime juice

> 1 tablespoon lime zest

> ¼ cup tequila

> 1 teaspoon cracked black pepper

> 1 tablespoon soya sauce

> 1 tablespoon Worcestershire sauce

> 1 tablespoon fresh cilantro, minced

> ½ cup dark brown sugar

> salt to taste

Grilled Tuna

Although fishers in New Brunswick don't bring home tuna, we still love to serve it. Tuna is a firm fish that lends itself to the barbecue nicely.

Ingredients

- 2 pounds fresh tuna fillets

- ½ cup butter

- 1 tablespoon cayenne pepper

- 1 teaspoon garlic powder

- ½ teaspoon salt

- 1 teaspoon black pepper

- Lemon or lime wedges (optional).

Method

1. Wash and pat dry tuna fillets and set aside.

2. Melt butter over low heat and add all seasonings.

3. Place tuna onto hot barbecue and baste often with butter mixture. Turn over only once and repeat. Cook for 8–10 minutes per side. The fish will be plump and the colour will change from red to white once cooked.

Serves 2–4

The 1972 record for the largest tuna fish ever caught was held by Guy Blanchard and Roger Dugas of Grande-Anse on the Acadian Peninsula. It weighed 800 pounds. That record was washed away by Camille J. Blanchard of Caraquet in 1976 when he caught a 1,130-pounder!

Grilled Halibut

Method

1. Wash fish, set aside.

2. Mix salt, pepper, garlic, onion, lemon juice, plum sauce, and cherry tomatoes in a shallow dish.

3. Place fish in sauce, cover, and refrigerate for at least 2 hours (overnight is best, if possible).

4. Remove fish, but reserve marinade.

5. Wrap fish in foil and barbecue for about 10 minutes per side.

6. While the fish cooks, boil marinade in a small pot to reduce it for a sauce to serve over the fish.

Serves 2–4

Ingredients

> 2 pounds halibut steaks

> 1 teaspoon salt

> 1 teaspoon white pepper

> 1 clove garlic, minced

> ¼ cup onion, minced

> ¼ cup lemon juice

> 1 cup plum sauce

> 1 pint cherry tomatoes, cut into quarters

From the Sea

Lemon Grilled Trout

Ingredients

> 1 whole trout whole, cleaned

> salt and pepper to taste

> 2 lemons, sliced

> ½ cup lemon juice

Method

1. Pat dry the inside of the fish.

2. Sprinkle the inside with salt and pepper.

3. Place the sliced lemons evenly throughout the cavity of the fish.

4. Wrap fish with tinfoil so the head and tail are sticking out and poke a few holes in the foil.

5. Bake on the barbecue (approximately 10 minutes per inch of length).

6. Let sit 5 minutes before opening.

7. Remove foil and lemon pieces, sprinkle with lemon juice as soon as you unwrap it, then slice and serve.

New Brunswick has many rivers and streams. Hidden within their fresh waters are speckled trout, and every fisher has their favourite spot to catch them.

Sweet 'n' Sour Barbecue Shrimp

Method

1. In a deep bowl, mix all ingredients (except shrimp) and set aside.

2. Place shrimp in sauce and marinate for 30 minutes.

3. Remove shrimp, but reserve marinade.

4. Boil the marinade to cook off any raw fish juice. Reduce by one-third over medium heat.

5. Place shrimp on the barbecue and baste constantly with the reduced marinade until shrimp are pink and tightly curled, about 5 minutes per shrimp. Turn only once during cooking.

Serves 2–4

Ingredients

› 2 pounds raw shrimp, shelled and de-veined

› 1 cup Italian-style salad dressing

› ¼ cup brown sugar

› 2 cups crushed pineapple

› 2 cloves garlic, minced

› salt and pepper to taste

From the Sea

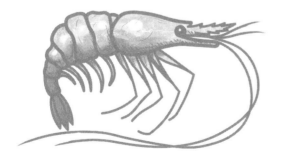

Parmesan Fried Scallops

Ingredients

- 64 baby scallops (8 per skewer)

- 1 cup Parmesan cheese, grated

- ½ cup bread crumbs

- salt and pepper to taste

- 16 slices of bacon

- 16 wooden skewers or bamboo rods

- juice from 1 lemon* to garnish

Any citrus juice may be used: lime, lemon, orange, grapefruit, etc.

Method

1. In a small bowl, mix cheese, bread crumbs, salt, and pepper until even.

2. Spread crumbs on a cookie sheet. (You will be rolling the completed skewers in the crumbs.)

3. Thread 8 baby scallops on a skewer with a strip of bacon, weaving the bacon in between each scallop.

4. Roll each skewer in the crumb mixture, coating as much as possible.

5. Broil in the oven or grill on the barbecue until bacon is crispy. Approximately 10 to 20 minutes.

6. Sprinkle with fresh lemon juice before serving.

Serve 4–8

Barbecue Shrimp Skewers

Method

1. Wrap each shrimp in a piece of prosciutto and weave onto the skewer. Thread 3 shrimp per skewer.

2. Grill on high heat, sprinkling with salt and pepper, until shrimp are pink and curled and proscitutto becomes crispy.

3. Serve with chutney or salsa.

Serves 4–8

Ingredients

› 2 pounds shrimp, cleaned and de-veined

› ½ pound prosciutto, sliced as thinly as possible

› black pepper to taste

From the Sea

When using wooden skewers, soak them in water for at least 30 minutes before use. This will prevent them from burning. The water also makes the skewers a little softer, so be gentle when piercing food pieces. (You can cut wooden sticks in half for appetizer-sized skewers.) Bamboo skewers are a little sturdier than wood and don't splinter as easily.

Metal rods are generally bigger in size and hold more food. The metal version also heats from the inside out and continues to hold its temperature for a few minutes once removed from the heat—be careful when handling!

Summer Shrimp Kebabs

Try serving these tasty seafood skewers with Summer Corn Salsa (recipe on page 134) for a light and fresh meal.

Ingredients

- 8 wooden skewer sticks or bamboo rods

- 24 large shrimp, butterfly cut*

- 24 whole baby white onions, peeled

- 24 pineapple, cut into 1-to-2-inch wedges

- 3 limes, cut into 8 wedges each

- 24 whole baby mushrooms

- 24 red pepper pieces, cut into 1-inch squares

- salt and pepper to taste

See page 39 for instructions on cleaning and preparing butterfly shrimp, but keep in mind this is only a suggestion for aesthetic purposes.

Method

1. Thread each skewer with at least 3 of each ingredient. Alternate shrimp, then fruit, then vegetable. Place a wedge of lime next to pieces of shrimp at all times.

2. Place on middle rack in barbecue (with cover closed) or in the oven at 425° and cook for 15 minutes, or until shrimp are pink and tightly curled.

3. Serve hot on a bed of rice, in a pita pocket, on a flour tortilla, or as a portion of a larger meal.

Hint: Save the shrimp shells to make a lovely seafood stock (see page 55 for instructions).

Serves 4–8

Barbecued Stuffed Salmon

Method

1. Choose a salmon that is big enough to feed your crowd (about 2 inches per person).

2. Clean salmon, remove the head and tail. (You can leave head and tail on for decoration if you like.) Slice the fish open along the belly and remove the backbone. Discard innards and set fish aside.

3. In a deep bowl, combine the rest of the ingredients, mixing well.

4. Stuff salmon, being certain not to overstuff.

5. Wrap salmon loosely in tinfoil.

6. Cook approximately 2 hours, either in an oven at 350°, or on the upper rack of a barbecue that has reached 350°.

7. Let salmon sit for 10 minutes before unwrapping to retain the natural moisture.

Campbellton is famous for its salmon from the Restigouche River. They celebrate each year with local cultural festivities. Try some salmon; cold smoked, maple cured or just thrown on the barbecue. This region is also well known for its exceptional winter skiing adventures.

Ingredients

- 1 whole salmon
- 4 cups bread crumbs
- ½ cup almonds, ground
- ¼ cup almonds, sliced
- ¼ cup pistachios
- 1 ½ cups onion, minced
- ½ cup red pepper, minced
- ¼ cup green pepper, minced
- 3 cloves garlic, minced
- ½ cup apple, peeled and minced
- ¼ cup butter, melted
- ¼ cup lemon juice
- salt and pepper to taste

MAINS

Strawberry Snow Crab

Ingredients

> 16 large crab legs, scrubbed

> 1 cup whole strawberries, rinsed with stems removed

> ¼ cup white sugar

> 2 cups cold water

> 1 tablespoon soya sauce

> 1 tablespoon Worcestershire sauce

> 1 lemon, sliced

Method

1. Place all ingredients except for crab in a deep pot and stir well until sugar is dissolved.

2. Place crab legs on top of mixture, making sure the open ends of legs are on top, facing up.

3. Cover the pot and bring to a boil.

4. Reduce heat to low and simmer 10 minutes, covered.

Suggestion: Serve with melted butter. Reserve berry mixture for dipping.

Serves 4–6

Cod Florentine

Method

1. Preheat oven to 350°.

2. Place all of the ingredients (except for the tomatoes and cod), into a food processor and blend until creamy.

3. Fold in the diced tomatoes. Set aside.

4. Clean fillets and lay flat. Spread approximately 1 to 3 tablespoons of filling onto each fillet, then roll each one up like a log.

5. Place in a shallow baking dish with 1 inch between each fillet.

6. Bake for 20 minutes until fish is firm.

Hint: You may like to serve this dish with a sauce like hollandaise, béchamel (page 113), or cheese sauce.

Ingredients

> 2 pounds cod fillets

> 1 cup ricotta or cottage cheese

> 2 cups spinach, rinsed and chopped

> ½ cup pistachios*

> 1 tablespoon onion, minced

> 1 tablespoon celery, minced

> 1 clove garlic, minced

> 1 teaspoon chili powder

> ½ teaspoon dried dill

> salt and pepper to taste

> 1 cup green tomato, diced

Use any type of nut you prefer, like pine nuts, almonds, cashews, pecans, walnuts, etc.

Atlantic Deep Dish Salmon Pie

Ingredients

- 2 Perfect Pie Crust (recipe on page 176)

- 2 pounds salmon, cleaned, cooked, and flaked

- ¼ cup onion, minced

- ¼ cup celery, minced

- ½ cup red pepper, minced

- 1 cup green tomato, chopped

- 1 clove garlic, minced

- 1 tablespoon lemon juice

- 2 tablespoon butter, melted

- 1 cup sour cream

- 1 tablespoon Worcestershire sauce

- ½ teaspoon dried basil

- 1 cup bread crumbs

- 2 tablespoons Parmesan cheese, grated (optional)

Method

1. Preheat oven to 375°.

2. Prepare pie crust and grease a deep-dish pie plate. Place bottom half of pastry into pie plate.

3. In a deep bowl, combine all of the remaining ingredients gently and stir gently until evenly mixed. Spread into the pie shell.

4. Cover with top half of pie shell. Press edges of both crusts together. Use a fork and to pierce vent holes in top layer.

5. Bake for 30 to 45 minutes, or until crust is golden.

6. (*Optional*) When the pie is ready to come out of the oven cover it with freshly grated Parmesan cheese and replace in oven until melted.

Serves 6–8

Sautéed Garlic Shrimp with Sweet Peppers

Method

1. Heat oil in a large frying pan, add onions and garlic, and sauté over medium heat, stirring constantly, for about 3 minutes.

2. Add shrimp and toss. As soon as the shrimp start to turn pink, add peppers, chili powder, salt, and pepper.

3. Cover and let steam over low heat for 5 minutes stirring frequently but gently. As soon as peppers turn tender, remove from heat.

Suggestion: Serve over Citrus Rice (recipe on page 77), or try it with the Three Cheese Potatoes (recipe on page 150).

Ingredients

> 1 tablespoon olive oil

> ½ cup onion, thinly sliced

> 1 bulb garlic, sliced thinly

> 2 pounds raw shrimp, cleaned and de-veined

> 1 cup red pepper, sliced

> 1 cup yellow pepper, sliced

> ½ teaspoon chili powder

> salt and pepper to taste

Traditional Fish Cakes

This recipe is the basic method for making codfish cakes, but I have also included instructions for other seafood varieties or combinations. The variations are based on which ingredients will complement each type of seafood or shellfish best.

Ingredients

- 4 cups cod*, cooked and flaked

- 2 cups mashed potatoes, cooled

- ¼ cup mayonnaise

- 1 tablespoon soya sauce

- ½ teaspoon dried dill

- 1 teaspoon lemon juice

- ¼ cup onion, grated

- 1 cup bread crumbs

- 1 egg, beaten

- 1 tablespoon Worcestershire sauce

- salt and pepper to taste

- ¼ cup clarified butter (recipe on page 2)

- 2 cups Cornflakes, crushed

Method

1. Clean fish of any bones (Most varieties of fish can be diced small; some, like salmon and crab, are better flaked.) Cover and set aside in fridge until ready to use.

2. Place potatoes in a deep bowl, mix in the mayonnaise, soya sauce, dill, lemon juice, onion, bread crumbs, egg, Worcestershire sauce, salt, and pepper. Fold in the seafood* and mix until evenly distributed.

*For each specific type of seafood, add the extra ingredients listed on the next page during step 2.

3. Use a ¼ measuring cup or ice cream scoop to portion out patties. Flatten and shape patties with your hands. (Use cold water or lightly grease your hands if the mixture becomes too sticky, or return mixture to the fridge for 30 minutes to stiffen up.)

Continued next page...

4. Place patties on a cookie sheet, and brush with clarified butter. Roll in crushed Cornflakes, then return to the cookie sheet. Bake for 30 minutes, or until golden and crispy. Alternatively, fry in oil for about 5 minutes per side, or until crispy.

Suggestion: These fish cakes may be served as a side dish, main, or made very small and served as hors d'oeuvres.

Serves 6–18, depending on size

*Seafood Variations:

Hungryman Halibut Fish Burger: (You could use haddock or sole as well.) Add 1 teaspoon lemon juice and ¼ cup sharp cheddar cheese, grated.

Crusty Crab Cakes: Add 2 tablespoons lemon juice, ¼ cup grated Swiss cheese, and ½ teaspoon nutmeg.

Zingy Salmon Circles: Add 2 tablespoons lemon juice, 1 teaspoon dried dill, and ½ teaspoon grated ginger root.

Succulent Scallop Snowballs: Add ½ cup sweetened shredded coconut, 2 tablespoons lime juice, and 1 teaspoon lime zest.

Luscious Lobster Medallions: Add 1 minced clove garlic, 1 teaspoon minced capers, 1 tablespoon lemon juice, and 4 slices of crumbled bacon.

The Bay of Fundy is the best visual experience you can walk through. The glacial carved rocks are formed from 100 billion tons of water which rise and fall as part of nature's power and grace of gravity. These rock formations are beautiful to look at.

A lobster's biggest claw is called the "crusher." The smaller claw is called the "pincher" claw, usually used for holding food and assisting the crusher claw. Lobsters with only one claw or no claws are called "culls," and are usually available for a lower price as they have less meat.

When at the local fish market selecting your lobster, choose females as they are usually larger, contain more meat, and are sweeter than the males. If the internal roe (eggs) are still intact, they may be reserved for a garnish on salad, soup, or on crackers.

In order to preserve the lobster industry, all fishers who catch a female lobster bearing eggs (referred to as "berried"), with her underside covered in bright red roe, must release the female back into the water. This is not just a good deed but a law in order to protect the many fishers who rely on a healthy lobster population.

Most scientists say lobsters have no cerebral cortex (the area of the brain that gives the perception of pain), thus they do not feel pain. Lobsters do not have vocal cords so they do not scream when you cook them. There is sometimes a hissing sound as steam escapes from their shell.

Shediac, New Brunswick, is known as the lobster capital of the world. When visiting New Brunswick, make sure to stop in Moncton during the month of August for their famous Atlantic Seafood Festival—it gets bigger every year.

Lobster Clubhouse Sandwich for Two

Method

1. In a small bowl, place lobster and sprinkle with lemon juice, salt, and pepper. Stir well until lemon juice is soaked up.

2. Fry bacon until crispy, discard grease, and pat dry.

3. Spread one slice of bread with some tartar sauce. Add the cheese, bacon, lettuce, tomato, and lobster. Spread the second slice of bread with tartar sauce and place on top of the filling. Repeat for second sandwich.

Serves 2

Ingredients

> 1 pound lobster meat (claws, knuckles, or tails), chopped

> 1 teaspoon lemon juice

> salt and pepper to taste

> 4 slices bacon

> 4 slices bread

> ¼ cup tartar sauce

> ¼ cup cheddar cheese, grated

> 2 leaves lettuce

> 8 slices tomato

Sailor's Breakfast Omelette

Ingredients

> ½ pound maple-cured bacon

> 3 large eggs

> salt and pepper to taste

> 1 tablespoon maple syrup

> ½ cup salmon, cooked, cooled, and flaked

> 1 cup potatoes, peeled, cooked, and diced

> 1 tablespoon fresh chives, minced

> ½ cup sharp cheddar cheese, grated

Method

1. Fry bacon until crispy, pat it dry, then crumble. Reserve fat in the pan and set bacon aside.

2. In a small bowl, beat eggs until frothy, sprinkle with salt and pepper.

3. Add maple syrup, salmon, and potatoes. Stir until evenly mixed.

4. Pour mixture into frying pan with bacon grease, and cook over medium to high heat.

5. Stir for 1 minute and then let rest, covering immediately and reducing heat to low.

6. Let omelette cook for 2 to 3 minutes. Add bacon, chives, and cheese. Cover again and turn off heat.

7. As soon as cheese is melted, serve piping hot.

Serves 1–2

Maritime Lobster Croissant

Method

1. Mix mayonnaise, green onion, lemon juice, mustard, celery, and the lobster together in a bowl until evenly mixed. Cover and refrigerate.

2. Slice the croissant in half and spread insides with garlic butter.

3. Fry buttered-side down in a frying pan or broil buttered-side up in the oven.

4. Place the lobster mixture on the bottom half of the croissant. Top with shredded cheese.

5. Place under broiler in oven to melt. Top with other half of croissant and serve.

Serves 1

Ingredients

- 3 ounces lobster meat, cleaned and chopped

- 1 croissant

- 1 teaspoon mayonnaise*

- 1 teaspoon green onion, minced

- ½ teaspoon lemon juice

- 1 teaspoon mustard

- 1 teaspoon celery, minced

- 1 tablespoon garlic butter

- ¼ cup shredded cheese of choice

You can substitute the mayonnaise for ranch dressing, sour cream, or any other condiment you prefer.

From the Sea

The Shediac Lobster Festival is an opportunity for all to toast this delectable delicacy. Revellers also make time to enjoy the wonderful sand and surf at Parlee Beach.

Codfish Crumpets

Try placing some scrambled egg on the top half and serve this dish open-faced.
Or be extravagant and serve with a cheese or hollandaise sauce over top.

Ingredients

> 4 cod fillets

> 2 tablespoons olive oil

> ¼ cup onion, minced

> 4 crumpets, sliced

> 4 tablespoons cream cheese*

> 1 cup cheddar cheese*, grated

Try a herbed cream cheese, or swap the cheddar cheese for Swiss or mozzarella to play with the flavour.

Method

1. Preheat oven to 400°.

2. In a large frying pan, heat oil and fry cod over medium heat until fully cooked. Pat dry and set aside.

3. Drain oil from pan and fry onion until tender. Remove from heat.

4. Lightly toast the crumpets, then place 4 bottom halves on a cookie sheet.

5. Spread 1 tablespoon of cream cheese on each crumpet. Spoon onion on top.

6. Place a fish portion on top of the onion and sprinkle with cheddar cheese.

7. Bake until cheese is bubbly. Top with the other half of toasted crumpet and serve hot.

Serves 4

Atlantic Salmon Patties

Method

1. Combine all ingredients (except oil) in a large bowl, mixing well.

2. Form into round patties about 1 inch thick.

3. Heat oil in a frying pan and fry patties until crisp.

Serves 4–6

Ingredients

- 2 pounds salmon, cooked, cleaned, and flaked

- 4 cups mashed potatoes

- ¼ cup flour

- 1 tablespoon onion, minced

- 1 tablespoon celery, minced

- ½ cup bread crumbs

- ¼ cup Parmesan cheese, grated

- ¼ cup bacon bits

- 2 cloves garlic, minced

- ¼ cup melted butter

- salt and pepper to taste

- 1 tablespoon olive oil

Sides and Such

Lemon-Thyme Roasted Tomato Sauce

Use this sauce as a marinade or basting sauce, or as a base for pizza or bruschetta. Chicken and potatoes baked in this sauce are out of this world!

Ingredients

› 2 pounds fresh tomatoes*

› 2 lemons (1 sliced, 1 zested)

› 1 tablespoon dried basil

› 1 teaspoon dried thyme

› ¼ cup olive oil

› salt and pepper to taste

Tomatoes can be of any variety, such as baby, plum, beefsteak, cherry, heirloom, or field. The quantity and size of the tomato will change based on what variety you use. Different tomatoes have different amounts of seeds, juice, and pulp. Experiment with what you can find in your area. I prefer plum tomatoes for this recipe.

Method

1. Cut tomatoes in half and place them in a shallow baking dish.

2. Seed and cut 1 lemon into 12 slices. Place them amongst the tomatoes. Set aside.

3. In a small bowl mix basil, thyme, and zest with oil, then pour over the tomatoes.

4. Bake at 325° until the tomatoes are soft, about 15 to 45 minutes depending how hot your oven is.

5. Let cool. Remove and discard lemon slices.

6. Place everything into a food processor and purée for 4 minutes. You can strain through a fine sieve for a smoother sauce. Serve warm or cold.

Makes 2 cups

Mustard Tarragon Glaze

Use this tangy sauce for dipping, baking, or basting.

Method

1. Whisk everything together in a bowl.

2. Cover and refrigerate for 1 hour before using to allow flavours to develop and blend.

Makes approximately 3 cups

Ingredients

> 1 cup sour cream

> ½ cup plain yogurt

> ½ cup honey mustard

> ½ cup whole-grain mustard

> ¼ cup regular mustard

> 1 tablespoon lemon juice

> 1 tablespoon lime juice

> 2 tablespoons fresh tarragon, minced (or 1 teaspoon dried)

> salt and pepper to taste

Herbed Churned Butter

Ingredients

- 2 cups butter

- 2 tablespoons parsley

- 2 tablespoons garlic minced plus 1 tablespoon parsley

- 2 tablespoons mint

- 2 tablespoons basil

- 2 tablespoons rosemary

- 1 teaspoon coriander

- 1 teaspoon cinnamon

- 2 teaspoon cayenne pepper

- 2 teaspoon chili powder

- ½ cup crushed berries (strawberries, cranberries, or blueberries)

Method

1. Whip butter for 2 minutes.

2. Add one or more of the suggested seasonings and beat again for 1 minute.

Hint: Use as a spread for toast, when frying meat or vegetables, or for basting.

White Sauce (Béchamel)

This sauce can be used in a variety of ways, but is best in a dish that needs a bit more moisture or creaminess, but not a lot of extra flavour.

Method

1. In a sauce pan, melt butter over low heat. Slowly sprinkle in the flour, and whisk until all is absorbed by the butter. Mixture may look crumbly or doughy.

2. Continue whisking and slowly add the milk. Stir constantly until smooth.

3. Gradually increase the heat to medium, and keep stirring until mixture begins to thicken. Once the mixture becomes as thick as corn syrup, remove from heat. Sprinkle with salt and pepper. Stir.

4. Remember: once you remove the sauce from the stove, is will still be hot and continue to thicken for a minute or so. This sauce is best used right away, because after it cools it may need to be thinned when reheating.

Hint: For a flavoured white sauce, add any one or combination of these items as soon as you remove sauce from heat: curry, 1 teaspoon; fresh parsley, 1 tablespoon; mushroom, 1 cup cooked and minced; onion, ½ cup cooked and minced; dill, 1 tablespoon; mustard, 2 tablespoons; ½ cup cranberries (crushed or whole) plus 1 tablespoon brown sugar.

Ingredients

> 3 tablespoons butter

> 6 tablespoons flour

> 1 cup milk

> salt and pepper to taste

Cheese Sauce

Serve this sauce over steamed fresh vegetables, tossed with pasta, or on top of a fish or chicken dish.

Ingredients

- 2 tablespoons butter

- 2 tablespoons flour

- ½ teaspoon mustard

- 1 cup milk

- 2 to 3 cups cheddar* cheese, grated

- salt and pepper to taste

Substitute any variety of cheese you prefer (Swiss, mozzarella, Parmesan)

Method

1. In a saucepan, melt butter with mustard on low heat.

2. Add flour and stir until all flour is absorbed. Mixture may look crumbly or doughy.

3. Slowly add milk, stirring constantly until smooth.

4. Increase heat to high, stirring constantly, until the sauce begins to thicken.

5. When the desired thickness is achieved, turn off the heat and quickly stir in the cheese, stirring until the cheese is completely melted. Sprinkle in salt and pepper.

6. Serve immediately. This sauce can be made ahead, but will be a little thinner when reheated.

Makes approximately 1 ½ cups

Hint: In step 5, you can add some optional flavours: Worcestershire sauce, soya cause, fresh-snipped herbs (parsley, basil, or thyme), hot peppers, or salsa.

Creamy Peppercorn Sauce

This sauce is delicious served over steak or chicken. It also lends itself well to baked dishes, or as a flavouring for gravy.

Method

1. In a pot, combine cream, peppercorns, wine, chicken stock powder, mustard, and Worcestershire sauce. Stir over low heat.

2. Increase heat until mixture comes to a boil, then reduce heat until the mixture is just under a boil.

3. In a small bowl, mix cornstarch and water and gradually whisk into the cream mixture, stirring constantly.

4. Remove from heat and add chives, salt, and pepper.

Makes approximately 1 cup

Ingredients

> 1 ¼ cups whipping cream

> 2 tablespoon green or black peppercorns

> 2 tablespoons white wine

> 1 teaspoon chicken stock powder

> 1 teaspoon mustard

> 1 tablespoon Worcestershire sauce

> 2 teaspoons cornstarch

> 3 tablespoons cold water

> 1 tablespoon chives or green onions, chopped

> salt and pepper to taste

Alfredo Sauce

Ingredients

- 1 cup milk

- 1 cup whipping cream

- 1 tablespoon garlic butter

- 1 teaspoon parsley

- salt and pepper to taste

- ½ cup Parmesan cheese

Method

1. Bring all of the ingredients except cheese to a boil on medium to high heat without burning the milk. Stir constantly.

2. As the liquid is boiling, add ½ cup Parmesan cheese and continue to stir constantly. Cheese will thicken the sauce instantly. Remove from heat and use immediately as a sauce or a base for a casserole.

Makes approximately 2 cups

Roasted Garlic

Use any oil remaining in the baking dish for cooking,
as it will have a nice full-bodied flavour.

Ingredients

> 6 whole bulbs garlic

> ½ cup olive oil

> salt and pepper to taste

Method

1. Preheat oven to 300°.

2. Slice ½ inch off the top of each garlic bulb, expos-ing the middle. Make sure to cut as flat as possible so your bulb, when sitting, does not lean to one side.

3. Place cut bulbs and their tops in a shallow baking dish.

4. Drizzle olive oil over making sure all parts are evenly coated. Sprinkle with salt and pepper.

5. Cover and bake for 25 to 45 minutes, or until the cloves have softened. The cloves will start to look transparent and will start to lift themselves out of the bulb a little.

6. Remove from oven and spread on toasted rounds or use in other recipes. Store in fridge, in an airtight container, for up to 2 weeks.

Variation: Try Sweet Roasted Garlic! Prepare as above, substituting oil, salt, and pepper with ½ cup butter and ½ cup brown sugar. Cream together and spread on bulbs prior to baking.

Homemade Caesar Salad Dressing

This is a wonderful creamy dressing for salads, a delicious dipping sauce for vegetables, or a great accompaniment for meat dishes.

Ingredients

- 2 cups mayonnaise
- 1 cup olive oil
- ⅔ cup white vinegar
- ¼ cup lemon juice
- 3 cloves garlic, minced
- 2 tablespoons dried oregano
- salt and pepper to taste

Method

1. In a small bowl or blender, mix all ingredients until smooth and even.

2. Cover and refrigerate. Let sit overnight before using to allow flavours to blend and strengthen.

Hint: If you use garlic powder instead of fresh garlic, the dressing will keep longer and be stronger in flavour, as the powder is more concentrated. (1 teaspoon is all you need!)

Makes approximately 1 litre

Apple Vinaigrette

Use this vinaigrette as a salad dressing, or as a marinade or condiment for fish, chicken, or pork dishes.

Method

1. Purée all ingredients in a food processor or blender until smooth, about 3 minutes. Strain through a fine sieve.

2. Store in the refrigerator for up to 1 month in an airtight jar. Shake before using.

Makes 2 cups

Variations: In place of the applesauce, substitute one (or a combination) of the following:

Cranberry Vinaigrette: 2 cups cranberries

Raspberry Rapture: 2 cups raspberries

Blueberry Blue Sauce: 2 cups blueberries

Strawberry Slather: 2 cups strawberries

Blackberry Drizzle: 2 cups blackberries

> *Pennfield, located between Saint John and St. Stephen, is the home to bountiful blueberry fields. U-pick farms offer the chance to select berries for your favourite recipe.*

Ingredients

> 2 cups applesauce*

> ¼ cup olive oil

> ¼ cup vinegar

> 1 teaspoon lemon juice

> 1 teaspoon lemon zest

> salt and pepper to taste

*Use homemade applesauce for best flavour, but you can also use jam, jelly, frozen (thaw first), or freshly mashed apples.

Raspberry Balsamic Glaze

Use this glaze as a basting sauce, marinade, salad dressing, or dip.

Ingredients

> 2 cups fresh raspberries

> ½ cup balsamic vinegar

> 1 tablespoon honey

> pinch of salt

> ½ teaspoon black pepper

Method

1. Place all ingredients in a thick-bottomed saucepan and simmer over medium heat, stirring often, for about 15 minutes, or until raspberries fall apart.

2. Remove from heat, let cool.

3. Purée or mash until smooth. Strain through a fine sieve to produce a thick, smooth liquid.

4. Store in the refrigerator for up to 1 month in an airtight jar.

Makes approximately 1 cup

Variation: Try using a different fruit or combination of fruits like blueberries, strawberries, cranberries, blackberries, Granny Smith or McIntosh apples.

SAUCES, GLAZES, & DRESSINGS

Chicken Ball Sauce

Method

1. In a thick-bottomed pot, combine all ingredients and stir. Simmer for 10 minutes over medium heat.

2. Use a cornstarch-based thickener (if desired) to achieve desired thickness.

Makes approximately 1 cup

Ingredients

> ¼ cup vinegar

> 1 cup water

> ½ cup pineapple* juice

> 1 tablespoon soya sauce

> ¼ cup ketchup

> ¼ cup brown sugar

Try using orange, apple, or cranberry juice instead of pineapple.

Sides & Such

Peanut Sauce

Peanut Sauce is a traditional condiment for many Thai recipes.

Ingredients

> 1 cup peanut butter (smooth or crunchy)

> 1 clove garlic, minced

> 1 tablespoon lemon juice

> 1 teaspoon cumin powder

> 1 teaspoon fish sauce

> 1 teaspoon cayenne powder (optional)

Method

1. Mix all ingredients in a bowl until incorporated.

Makes approximately 1 cup

Classic Barbecue Sauce

Method

1. In a deep saucepan, combine all ingredients and cook over medium heat, stirring often, for about 15 minutes.

2. Reduce heat to low and simmer for 15 additional minutes.

3. Remove from heat and store in the refrigerator for up to 1 month in an airtight jar.

Makes approximately 2 cups

Ingredients

- ¼ cup onion, minced
- ¼ cup celery, minced
- 1 clove garlic, minced
- ½ cup brown sugar
- ½ cup apple cider vinegar
- 1 tablespoon lemon juice
- ½ cup ketchup
- ¼ cup chili sauce
- ¼ cup Worcestershire sauce
- ½ teaspoon dry mustard
- 1 teaspoon cayenne powder
- salt and pepper to taste

Basil Oil

Use this fresh-tasting oil for salad dressing, cooking oil,
a dip for fresh bread, or drizzled on pizza.

Ingredients

> 2 cups fresh basil leaves
> (tightly packed)

> 2 cups olive oil

Method

1. Place basil and oil in a food processor or blender and purée for about 2 minutes.

2. Strain mixture through cheesecloth or a fine sieve to remove all leaf particles. (This is not necessary if you like the basil chunks, but they will burn if using this oil for cooking.)

3. Store in the refrigerator for up to 1 month in an airtight jar.

Variations: In place of basil, substitute one (or a combination) of the following:

Mint: 1 cup fresh mint leaves—excellent for Greek-style dishes featuring lamb, and for desserts.

Ginger: 1 cup grated ginger root—perfect for Thai-style dishes and pork.

Thyme: 1 cup fresh thyme leaves—creates a Greek-style flavour; try with chicken.

Rosemary: 1 cup fresh rosemary leaves—ideal for Mediterranean dishes with lamb, chicken, or pork.

Raspberry Maple Syrup

Goes great over oatmeal, pancakes, or French toast, but give this syrup a try on ice cream, cheesecake, or pie too!

Method

1. Pour maple syrup into a deep bowl. Add all remaining ingredients and stir until evenly mixed.

2. Store in an airtight jar in the refrigerator for up to 1 month.

*Variations: Substitute one or a combination of the fruits listed below.

  Blueberry: Add 1 cup fresh blueberries mashed, or frozen (thaw first).

  Strawberry: Add 1 cup fresh strawberries mashed, or frozen (thaw first).

  Cranberry: Add 1 cup cranberries mashed, or frozen (thaw first).

  Autumn Apple: Add 1 cup applesauce.

Makes approximately 2 cups

Ingredients

> 1 cup maple syrup

> 1 cup fresh raspberries*

> 1 teaspoon cinnamon

> 1 teaspoon nutmeg

> pinch of salt

Roasted Red Pepper Dip

Serve this versatile dish as a vegetarian side, tossed with pasta,
spread on toasted bread rounds, or as a dip for vegetables.

Ingredients

> 2 pounds roasted red peppers*, minced

> ½ cup sweet onion, minced

> 2 cloves garlic, minced

> ¼ cup sesame oil

> ¼ cup sesame seeds

> 1 tablespoon soya sauce

> 1 tablespoon Worcestershire sauce

> salt and pepper to taste

> 2 cups soft cheese (such as ricotta, goat, or feta)

Roasted red peppers can be found in cans or jars in any grocery store. They have already been fire-roasted and become very sweet. You can also make your own (recipe on page 137).

Method

1. Preheat oven to 325°.

2. Place the roasted red peppers in a shallow 9 x 9 baking dish. Sprinkle with onion and garlic.

3. Sprinkle with the sesame oil, seeds, soya sauce, Worcestershire sauce, salt, and pepper.

4. Sprinkle with cheese and bake for 20 minutes, or until cheese is bubbly and golden .

5. Let cool slightly and serve warm.

Makes approximately 3–4 cups

Baked Brie

Method

1. Preheat oven to 325°.

2. Place an empty glass baking dish in the oven for 20 minutes to heat it up.

3. Heat the chutney in a small pot until hot and bubbly.

4. Place cheese into the preheated baking dish and top with heated chutney, spreading it out to cover the entire surface.

5. Cover dish immediately with plastic wrap or tinfoil and let stand for 3 minutes.

6. Uncover and serve with toasted bread rounds or crackers.

Serves 4–6

Ingredients

> 1 cup Rhubarb-Blackberry Chutney recipe (page 180)

> 1 (3-to-5-inch) wheel brie or Camembert cheese

Fiddlehead Dip 'n' Dunk

Serve this dish hot or cold as a dip, with chips and vegetables, or try it warm over pasta. It is sure to be a hit no matter how you serve it!

Ingredients

- 2 pounds fresh fiddleheads, rinsed thoroughly

- 1 cup apple juice

- ½ cup onion, finely minced

- 1 tablespoon soya sauce

- 1 tablespoon Worcestershire sauce

- 1 teaspoon white sugar

- 1 small clove garlic, minced

- 1 tablespoon lemon juice

- 1 teaspoon dried dill

- salt and pepper to taste

- 1 cup plain yogurt

- ½ cup sour cream

- ¼ cup mayonnaise

Method

1. Steam fiddleheads with apple juice until tender, about 3 to 5 minutes.

2. Submerge immediately in cold-water bath to stop the cooking process and retain the fiddleheads' bright green colour. Strain well.

3. Finely mince fiddleheads. Place in a deep bowl.

4. Add onion, soya sauce, Worcestershire sauce, sugar, garlic, lemon juice, dill, salt, and pepper. Stir for a few minutes until sugar is fully absorbed.

5. In a small bowl, mix the yogurt, sour cream, and mayonnaise. Add this creamy mixture to the main bowl, stir until even, and serve immediately.

Makes 2–3 cups

Sweet Fruit Dip

Method

1. Mix yogurt, sour cream, and marshmallow topping in a small bowl.

2. Cover and chill for 2 hours before serving.

3. Serve with sliced fruit.

Variation: Try Honeyed Fruit Dip! Prepare as above, substituting sour cream and marshmallow topping for ½ cup honey and cinnamon to taste.

Ingredients

> 1 cup yogurt, any flavour

> 1 cup sour cream

> 1 cup marshmallow topping (Fluff)

Creamy Blueberry Fruit Dunk

Use this versatile recipe as a fruit or vegetable dip, as a sauce to bake chicken or fish in, or as a dessert topping for pies, dumplings, and cheesecakes.

Ingredients

> 2 cups fruit* (jam, jelly, or freshly mashed)

> ½ cup sour cream

> ½ cup plain yogurt

> 2 tablespoons honey

> 1 tablespoon lemon juice

> ¼ teaspoon cinnamon

Method

1. Place all ingredients into a deep bowl and stir until evenly mixed.

2. Cover and refrigerate for 2 hours before using to allow flavours to blend. Stir before serving.

Makes approximately 3–4 cups

*Variations: In place of blueberries, substitute one (or a combination) of the following:

Raspberry Cream Dunk: 2 cups raspberries

Creamy Cranberry Sauce: 2 cups cranberries

Sweet Strawberry Sauce: 2 cups strawberries

Apple Cream Drizzle: 2 cups applesauce

Blackberry Dream Cream: 2 cups blackberries

Apple Walnut Wild Rice

Try this at room temperature over fresh spinach or lettuce as a rice salad!

Method

1. In a deep bowl, mix the white and wild rice until evenly distributed. Toss in the green onion, mix again, and set aside.

2. In a frying pan over medium heat, melt the butter. Fry the sweet onion for 3 minutes until tender.

3. Add mushrooms, stirring constantly. Sauté until the mushrooms are golden brown, about 5 to 10 minutes.

4. Add everything else except for the rice and stir-fry for 2 more minutes.

5. Add rice and keep stirring until rice is hot enough to serve.

Serves 4–8

Ingredients

> 1 cup wild rice, cooked and cooled

> 2 cups white long-grain rice, cooked and cooled

> ¼ cup green onion, chopped

> 2 tablespoons butter

> ½ cup sweet onion, minced

> 1 cup mushrooms, sliced

> 1 cup Granny Smith or McIntosh apple, minced

> ½ cup walnut pieces, roasted*

> ¼ cup soya sauce

> 1 tablespoon Worcestershire sauce

> salt and pepper to taste

*To roast walnuts, place the raw nuts on a cookie sheet and bake for 5 to 10 minutes on 350° or until you can smell the nuts. Remove from oven, salt if desired, and let cool.

Classic Italian Bruschetta

Ingredients

> 3 pounds tomatoes roughly chopped (baby, grape, cherry, or plum varieties)

> 1 cup olive oil

> ½ cup balsamic vinegar

> 1 bulb garlic, minced

> 1 cup onion, minced

> 1 tablespoon dried oregano

> 1 tablespoon fresh basil, chopped

> salt and pepper to taste

> 1 to 2 loaves baguette

Method

1. Preheat oven to 325°.

2. Place all ingredients (except bread) in a 9 x 13 glass casserole dish. Set casserole dish on a cookie sheet to provide an insulated bottom.

3. Bake for 1 hour, stirring a few times during cooking.

4. Serve slightly warm on toasted baguette rounds.

Store vegetable topping in an airtight container in the fridge for up to 2 weeks.

Makes approximately 3 cups

There are many varieties of basil to try, such as Genovese, Napolitano, sweet, cinnamon, lemon, bush, clove, Thai, licorice, holy, camphor, opal, purple, red, anise, and many more. Basil (fresh or dried) is a wonderful and popular compliment to tomatoes.

Curried Indian Rice

Method

1. Prepare rice according to package instructions. Fluff with a fork and set aside to cool.

2. In a large deep frying pan, melt butter and sauté the garlic, onion, and ginger for 3 minutes.

3. Add the tomatoes and fry for 2 minutes, stirring constantly.

4. Add curry powder, Worcestershire sauce, soya sauce, and lime juice. Sprinkle with salt and pepper and cook for 2 additional minutes.

5. Reduce heat to low, add rice to frying pan, and stir until rice is coated and heated through.

Hint: You may add the reserved tomato pulp to step 3 if you like (you may wish to strain it first to remove any seeds).

Serves 4–8

Ingredients

- 3 cups basmati rice, uncooked

- ¼ cup clarified butter (recipe on page 2)

- 1 clove garlic, minced

- ½ cup onion, minced

- 1 teaspoon fresh ginger root, grated

- 1 cup firm plum tomatoes, diced (pulp removed and reserved)

- 1 tablespoon curry power

- 1 tablespoon Worcestershire sauce

- 2 tablespoons soya sauce

- ½ cup lime juice

- salt and pepper to taste

Sides & Such

Summer Corn Salsa

Ingredients

- 6 ears of corn on the cob
- 2 whole red peppers
- 1 cup onion, diced small
- ½ cup green onion, diced small
- 1 cup zucchini, diced small
- 1 tablespoon fresh parsley, chopped
- 1 tablespoon olive oil
- 2 tablespoons lemon juice
- reserved red pepper juice

Method

1. Blacken corn and red peppers on the barbecue over very high heat. The corn will take 5 to 10 minutes, but the red peppers may take longer so start them first.

2. Once you have charred the red peppers, place them in a bowl and cover immediately with plastic wrap. Set bowl aside so the peppers can sweat.

3. Continue cooking the corn, then remove from heat. Let cool and slice corn off the cob.

4. When red peppers have cooled, peel off the blackened skin and discard it; it should remove easily. Seed and dice peppers. Reserve as much of the juice from peppers as you can.

5. Place corn, red peppers, onions, zucchini, and parsley into a deep bowl.

6. In a separate bowl, mix olive oil, lemon juice, and reserved pepper juice until even. Pour over vegetables and mix well.

Makes approximately 3 cups (serves 4–8)

Fruit Relish

Method

1. Place all ingredients into a small saucepan and heat on grill or stove top until it comes to a boil. Cook for 2 minutes more, stirring often. Remove from heat and pour over skewers.

Makes approximately 1 to 1 ½ cups

Ingredients

- ½ cup ripe mango, diced

- ½ cup firm avocado, diced

- ½ cup kiwi, diced

- 2 tablespoons lime juice

- 2 tablespoons lemon juice

- ¼ cup onion, minced

- 1 teaspoon garlic, minced

- 1 teaspoon Worcestershire sauce

- salt and pepper to taste

Did you know? Hartland in Carleton County boasts the longest covered bridge in the world. Built in 1901, it is 390 metres long. New Brunswick has many covered bridges but their number is dwindling. Fortunately their historical value and romantic appeal have led to efforts to preserve those that remain.

Sides & Such

No-Cook Pickles

Ingredients

- 3 pounds cucumbers, sliced as desired (thin, thick, peel on, or peel off)

- 1 cup onion, sliced round

- 2 to 4 cups white vinegar

- 2 teaspoons salt

- ½ teaspoon pepper

- 2 tablespoons white sugar

- 2 tablespoons fresh dill (plus sprigs for decoration)

- 1 clove garlic, minced

- ½ teaspoon mustard seed

Method

1. Wash cucumbers well, cut into desired shape, place in a large bowl, and sprinkle with salt. Let sit for 30 minutes and then drain off salt water, reserving the water in a separate bowl.

2. Mix everything else in a bowl. Add cucumbers.

3. Stir to distribute seasoning evenly and then taste mixture for salt content. Add salt water from cucumbers until desired taste is achieved.

4. In each bottle add the cucumbers, then fill the rest of the jar with ⅔ pure vinegar and ⅓ reserved pickle water. Add any seasonings like dill seed, dill weed, flakes, mustard seeds, etc. Cap bottles. Refrigerate for 24 hours before use for flavours to develop.

Makes approximately 4 cups

Roasted Red Peppers

Method

1. Preheat oven to 450°.

2. Rinse peppers but leave them whole. Place peppers in a cooking dish that can withstand high heat. Drizzle with oil, making sure to lightly coat all peppers. Sprinkle with salt and pepper.

3. Broil until peppers have blackened and look very burnt. Alternatively, grill on the barbecue over the highest heat. You could also use a kitchen blowtorch, if desired.

4. Once the outside skin has charred, remove peppers from heat. Place them in a dish and cover immediately with plastic wrap or tight-fitting lid so they can sweat.

5. Let peppers sit until cold, about 1 hour. Uncover and gently peel off the blackened skin. The skins should remove very easily at this point. Discard skins and seed peppers. You are left with sweet roasted peppers you can use in any dish. (Some blackened bits may remain, but this just adds a nice smoky flavour.)

Makes approximately 4 cups

Ingredients

> 2 pounds sweet or hot red peppers

> ½ cup olive oil

> salt and pepper to taste

Garlic Mashed Potatoes

Ingredients

- 1 teaspoon clarified butter (recipe on page 2)

- ¼ cup onion, minced

- 2 whole bulbs garlic, minced

- 5 pounds red- or yellow-skinned potatoes, peeled, cooked, and mashed

- ½ teaspoon white sugar

- ½ cup sour cream

- ½ cup heavy cream

- ¼ cup butter

- salt and pepper to taste

Method

1. In a large frying pan, melt clarified butter and sauté garlic and onion until golden. Set aside.

2. In a large mixing bowl, place mashed potatoes, sugar, sour cream, heavy cream, butter, salt, and pepper. Stir gently and fold in sautéed vegetables.

3. Using a hand mixer, whip potato mixture until light and fluffy, about 3 minutes.

4. Serve hot as a side dish, or cover and chill to use in other recipes.

Serves 4–10

Potatoes are the world's oldest known vegetable. New Brunswick farmers have been growing potatoes for over 100 years. They are sold domestically and exported internationally. We export to approximately 35 countries worldwide. The earliest record of potatoes being sold in New Brunswick dates back to the seventeenth century.

Herbed Corn on the Cob

Method

1. Preheat oven to 450° or barbecue to highest heat.

2. In a bowl, cream all ingredients except corn until smooth and even.

3. Husk corn and rinse cobs.

4. Using pastry brush, spread a thin layer of butter mixture over every piece of corn and place in a shallow baking dish.

5. Wrap each one snugly in tinfoil and cook for approximately 15 minutes.

Serves 10–12

Ingredients

- 12 ears corn

- 1 cup butter, softened (not melted)

- 2 tablespoons fresh parsley, chopped

- 1 tablespoon chives, minced

- 1 teaspoon dried thyme

- ½ teaspoon salt

- ¼ teaspoon cayenne powder

- 1 teaspoon black pepper

- ½ teaspoon garlic powder

- 1 tablespoon white sugar

Sides & Such

Irish Soda Bread

This is a great replacement for (or addition to) potatoes and goes well with gravy.

Ingredients

> 2 cups flour

> 1 tablespoon sugar

> 1 teaspoon baking powder

> ½ teaspoon salt

> 3 tablespoons butter

> 1 cup cold water

Method

1. Preheat oven to 400°.

2. In a deep bowl place all of the dry ingredients and stir so they are well mixed.

3. Cut in butter and use your hands to rub into flour mixture until the mixture resembles bread crumbs.

4. Add enough cold water (about ½ to ¾ cup) to stick dough together roughly so it is a little wet but not too dry. It should be slightly tacky.

5. Drape dough over roast beef, lamb, or pork.

6. Bake uncovered for 25 minutes until just slightly browned. Don't overcook or bread will crumble.

Irish immigrants swelled the population of New Brunswick in the 1800s. Descendants of these people are proud of their Irish roots. Each summer they gather to celebrate their heritage at the Irish Festival in Miramichi. The festival is held in summer and allows one and all to soak up Irish music, food, and culture.

Dough Boys or Dumplings

These bread-like additions to soups and stews can serve as an extra filler in the Saturday night soup pot. They can also take the place of potatoes in a stew.

Method

1. Sift all dry ingredients well in a large deep bowl.

2. Cut in butter and use your hands to rub into flour mixture until the mixture resembles bread crumbs.

3. Add enough cold water (about ½ to ¾ cup) to stick dough together roughly so it is a little wet but not too dry. It should be slightly tacky.

4. Drop by the spoonful into a liquid-based dish like soup or stew during the final 10 to 15 minutes of cooking time.

5. Cover pot tightly with a lid and let the dumplings steam. Do NOT lift the lid, as this will cause the dumplings to fall or not cook properly.

Ingredients

- 2 cups flour

- 1 tablespoon white sugar

- 2 teaspoons baking powder

- ½ teaspoon salt

- 2 tablespoon butter or margarine

- 1 cup cold water

Corned Beef Cakes

Ingredients

- 1 ½ pounds canned corned beef, rinsed

- 4 cups mashed potatoes, cooled

- ½ cup bread crumbs

- ¼ cup onion, minced

- 1 tablespoon celery, minced

- 1 clove garlic, minced

- 1 teaspoon soya sauce

Method

1. Break beef into pieces, removing any fat.

2. In a large bowl, mix beef and potatoes.

3. Add rest of ingredients, and stir until even.

4. Form into 2-inch patties.

5. In a non-stick or cast iron frying pan, fry patties until golden brown and crispy.

Serve with gravy.

Corned beef was a staple in old New Brunswick kitchens. It was a favourite of the Irish. You can almost catch a ghostly scent of corned beef and cabbage as you walk the streets of old Saint John.

Cranberry Yorkshire Pots

Goes great with chicken, turkey, pork, lamb, ham, or beef.

Method

1. Prepare Traditional Yorkshire Pudding according to instructions (recipe on page 144), using a muffin pan to make individual puddings. Do not bake.

2. In a small bowl, mix cranberries and cinnamon.

3. Place one heaping tablespoon of cranberry mixture on top of each uncooked pudding and bake at 400° for 45 to 60 minutes.

Serves 6–12

Ingredients

> 1 Traditional Yorkshire Pudding (recipe on page 144)

> 1 cup cranberries (freshly crushed, jelly, or jam)

> ¼ teaspoon cinnamon

Traditional Yorkshire Pudding

Ingredients

- 1 cup milk

- 2 eggs

- 1 cup flour

- ¼ teaspoon garlic powder

- 1 tablespoon soya sauce

- 1 tablespoon Worcestershire sauce

- salt and pepper to taste

- 1 cup meat drippings

Method

1. Preheat oven to 400°.

2. Combine milk, eggs, flour, garlic powder, soya sauce, Worcestershire sauce, salt, and pepper in a deep bowl.

3. Mix until smooth and well blended. Cover and refrigerate.

4. Lightly grease a 9 x 13 baking dish or muffin pan and pour in the meat drippings. Place in oven until pan is hot, about 5 to 10 minutes.

5. Remove pan from oven and add Yorkshire mixture. Return to oven and bake for 30 minutes.

Hint: You can prepare this mixture the night before and keep it in the fridge overnight. This allows the mixture to bind, thus producing a fluffier pudding.

...t Fry

...ossed with pasta or rice
...s an hors d'oeuvre.

Ingredients

> ¼ cup clarified butter
> (recipe on page 2)

> 2 pounds fresh fiddleheads,
> rinsed thoroughly

> 1 clove garlic, minced

> ¼ cup onion, minced

> 1 tablespoon lemon juice

> 1 tablespoon soya sauce

> 1 tablespoon Worcestershire
> sauce

> 1 cup raw cashews

> 1 tablespoon sesame seeds

> salt and pepper to taste

Garden Salad Croutons

Ingredients

> 1 tablespoon garlic powder

> 1 teaspoon dried basil

> ½ teaspoon chili powder

> 1 teaspoon dried oregano

> 1 teaspoon dried parsley

> salt and pepper to taste

> 3 cups bread, cubed

> ¼ cup olive oil

Method

1. In a small bowl, combine garlic, basil, chili powder, oregano, parsley, salt, and pepper.

2. In a separate, larger bowl, place the bread and sprinkle with the seasoning mixture. Stir a few times to ensure the bread is coated.

3. Add oil and stir.

4. Place in a non-stick frying pan or on a flat-top grill. Fry over medium heat until cubes become crispy, stirring often. Alternatively, bake at 250° for 20 minutes, stirring often to ensure even baking.

5. Serve on salad or soup. Store in an airtight container in a cool, dry place for up to 1 month.

Variations: Play with your flavour! Follow the same recipe above, but substitute these ingredients:

Lemon-Dill Croutons: ½ cup olive oil, ½ cup lemon juice, 1 tablespoon dried dill, 1 teaspoon soya sauce, 1 teaspoon Worcestershire sauce.

Garlic Croutons: ½ cup olive oil, ½ cup roasted garlic (recipe on page 117), 1 teaspoon soya sauce, 1 teaspoon Worcestershire sauce.

Potato Salad

New Brunswickers love picnics and potlucks, and
this popular salad travels well to either.

Method

1. In a large bowl, combine eggs, mayonnaise, and ranch dressing. Add the mashed potatoes and stir well until everything is evenly mixed.

2. Add the apple, corn, onion, celery, and garlic into the potatoes and stir again until evenly mixed.

3. Fold in the carrots and peas. Sprinkle with salt and pepper.

4. Place into a casserole dish, cover, and refrigerate until ready to serve.

Serves 15 as a side

New Brunswick is Canada's only officially bilingual province. Approximately one-third of the population speaks French. Acadian French is slightly different from that spoken in Quebec and France, reflecting a unique heritage.

Ingredients

> 6 eggs, hard-boiled, peeled, and mashed

> 1 cup mayonnaise

> ½ cup ranch salad dressing

> 5 pounds potatoes, peeled, cooked, mashed, and cooled

> 1 apple, cored and diced

> 1 cup corn, fresh or canned

> ½ cup onion, minced

> ½ cup celery, minced

> 1 clove garlic, minced

> 2 cups canned peas and carrots

> salt and pepper to taste

Picnic Coleslaw

Ingredients

- ½ cup mayonnaise
- 2 tablespoons sour cream
- ½ cup plain yogurt
- 1 tablespoon olive oil
- 1 tablespoon soya sauce
- 1 tablespoon Worcestershire sauce
- 2 tablespoons white vinegar
- 1 tablespoon white sugar
- 4 broccoli stems, grated
- 2 cups carrots, peeled and grated
- 2 cups green cabbage, grated
- ¼ cup onion, grated
- ¼ cup celery, grated
- salt and pepper to taste

Method

1. In a large salad bowl, mix mayonnaise, sour cream, yogurt, olive oil, soya sauce, Worcestershire sauce, vinegar, and sugar.

2. Add all the vegetables and toss until everything is evenly coated. Sprinkle with salt and pepper and stir.

3. Cover and refrigerate for 2 hours to allow the flavours to blend. Serve cold.

Serves 6–12

Savoury Stuffing

Method

1. Preheat oven to 325°.

2. Lightly grease a large casserole dish. Place bread cubes in dish. Add all vegetables and stir well to distribute evenly. Set aside.

3. In small bowl, mix the drippings, butter, poultry seasoning, sage, Worcestershire sauce, salt, pepper, and any additional herbs or spices you like until combined. Pour over bread and vegetables and toss well until evenly coated.

4. Bake until golden and crunchy, tossing every 20 to 30 minutes to ensure even cooking. This may take 1 to 3 hours, depending on the type of bread.

Makes approximately 6 cups

Suggestion: Serve with poultry or any meat any time of the year. This stuffing makes a great addition to the top of a steaming bowl of homemade chicken soup, or even on a salad as croutons.

Ingredients

- 6 cups bread, broken into 1-inch cubes

- 1 cup onion, diced

- 1 cup carrots, peeled and grated

- ½ cup mushrooms, sliced

- ½ cup celery, diced

- ½ cup meat drippings with fat (chicken, beef, or turkey)

- ½ cup butter, melted

- ¼ cup poultry seasoning

- 1 tablespoon sage

- 1 tablespoon Worcestershire sauce

- salt and pepper to taste

- seasoning of choice*

Use your favourite herbs (fresh or dried) such as rosemary, oregano, summer savoury, or parsley. Use 1 tablespoon fresh or 1 teaspoon dried.

Three Cheese Potatoes

Ingredients:

> 5 pounds potatoes, peeled, cubed, and cooked

> ½ cup Parmesan cheese, grated

> 1 (250-gram) block cream cheese

> ½ cup sour cream

> 2 tablespoons butter

> ½ cup cheddar cheese, grated

> salt and pepper to taste

Method:

1. Preheat oven to 400°.

2. In a large mixing bowl, place potatoes, Parmesan cheese, cream cheese, sour cream, and butter. Mash potatoes by hand, or use a hand-held mixer for extra-fluffy potatoes.

3. Place potato mixture in a shallow baking dish. Sprinkle with cheddar cheese, salt, and pepper.

4. Bake for 15 to 20 minutes, or until cheddar is melted and the tops of potatoes are brown and slightly crispy.

Four Bean Salad

If you do not like or have the beans listed, feel free to make substitutions like black beans, yellow wax beans, or navy beans.

Method:

1. In a large mixing bowl, place all vegetables and beans and stir gently to combine.

2. In a separate, smaller bowl, whisk together dressing ingredients until smooth. Pour over vegetables and toss to coat.

3. Cover and refrigerate for 24 hours before serving to allow flavours to develop and blend.

Hint: Canned foods are stored in a variety of liquids like water, seasoned water, salt brine, syrup, or broth. If you like the taste of the liquid you don't need to rinse the contents but if you prefer, you can rinse them under cold water.

Serves 6–10

Ingredients:

- 2 cups canned chickpeas
- 1 cup canned kidney beans
- 1 cup canned lima beans
- 1 cup canned white beans
- 1 cup onion, minced (red, white, or Vidalia)
- 1 cup red pepper, diced
- 1 cup green tomato, diced
- 1 cup cucumber, diced
- 1 cup zucchini, diced
- ½ cup green onion, sliced
- ½ cup fresh cilantro, chopped
- ¼ cup fresh mint, chopped

Dressing:

- 1 cup olive oil
- 1 cup sweet vinegar (red wine or apple cider)
- 1 teaspoon sesame oil
- 1 teaspoon lime zest
- 1 teaspoon lemon zest
- 1 tablespoon Worcestershire sauce
- 1 tablespoon soya sauce
- salt and pepper to taste

Sweet Coconut Rice

For an Asian flair, try adding 2 tablespoons of citrus zest to this creamy dish. Lemon, lime, grapefruit, or orange would all complement the coconut nicely!

Ingredients:

> 2 cups fragrant white rice (basmati or jasmine), uncooked

> 2 cups coconut milk

> ½ teaspoon cinnamon (optional)

> 1 teaspoon ground cardamom (optional)

> salt and pepper to taste

Method:

1. Prepare rice according to package directions substituting 2 cups of the required liquid with the coconut milk.

2. Fluff with a fork and add seasonings if desired.

Makes approximately 4 cups

Sweet Treats

Grandma's Classic Oatmeal Cookies

Try adding 1 to 2 cups of chocolate chips, raisins, dried cranberries, cherries, or blueberries after the oatmeal has been incorporated.

Ingredients

- 1 ¼ cups butter
- ¾ cup brown sugar
- ½ cup white sugar
- 1 egg
- 2 teaspoons vanilla
- 1 teaspoon baking soda
- 1 ½ cups flour
- 3 cups oatmeal (quick or minute oats)

Method

1. Preheat oven to 375°.

2. Cream butter and sugars until light and fluffy.

3. Add egg and vanilla and beat until incorporated.

4. Sift in dry ingredients (except oatmeal) and mix until smooth.

5. Add oatmeal and stir.

6. Drop by the tablespoon onto an ungreased or lined cookie sheet and bake for 8 to 12 minutes until just slightly golden around the edges. Remove from oven and let cookies rest for 5 minutes before removing them from cookie sheet. Cookies will keep in an airtight container for up to 1 week.

Hint: Overcooking will result in hard, crunchy cookies. These cookies should be a bit crisp on the edge and soft and chewy in the middle.

Makes 24 to 30 medium-sized cookies

Cherry Jubilee Shortbread

Method

1. Preheat oven to 350°.

2. Cream sugar and butter until light and fluffy. Add cherry juice and egg yolk and beat until smooth.

3. Stir in flour until dough is stiff and crumbly. Knead gently but do not overwork or your dough will be tough.

4. Roll into little balls and place on an ungreased cookie sheet about 1 inch apart. Flatten slightly with the back of a fork.

5. Place half a cherry in the centre of each cookie and bake for 10 to 12 minutes.

Hint: Cherries may be minced and added to the cookie dough for a more flavourful cherry taste and look. Add ¼ cup minced cherries at the end of step 2 and increase the flour by 2 tablespoons to absorb the extra moisture.

Ingredients

- 1 cup butter

- ¾ cup brown sugar

- 1 egg yolk

- 1 tablespoon cherry juice

- 2 cups white flour

- 1 cup maraschino cherries, sliced in half

Dream Cookies

Crust:

- 1 ½ cups graham cracker crumbs*

- 1 tablespoon white sugar

- ½ cup melted butter

Topping

- 2 cups milk chocolate chips

- 1 cup long sweetened coconut

- 1 cup nuts of choice (pecans, almonds, walnuts)

- 1 (14-ounce) can sweetened condensed milk

Shortbread may be used instead of graham cracker base if you prefer.

Method

1. Preheat oven to 350°.

2. Mix graham cracker crumbs with sugar and stir until even. Add melted butter and mix until sticky. Press firmly into a 9 x 13 baking dish.

3. Layer the topping ingredients in the following order: chocolate chips, coconut, nuts, and then the cream.

4. Bake for 20 to 45 minutes until golden and bubbly. Let cool and cut.

Peanut Butter Cookies

Method:

1. Preheat oven to 350°.

2. In a large mixing bowl, cream butter and sugars until light and fluffy.

3. Add egg and vanilla, beat until smooth.

4. Sift in flour, baking powder, salt, and nuts (if using) and stir until everything is incorporated.

5. Roll into 1-inch balls and place on an ungreased cookie sheet. Flatten balls slightly with the back of a fork.

6. Bake for 10 minutes and allow cookies to cool before transferring from cookie sheet to a wire cooling rack. Be careful not to overcook, or you will have tough, crunchy cookies!

Ingredients:

- ½ cup butter

- ½ cup peanut butter

- ½ cup white sugar

- ½ cup brown sugar

- 1 egg

- ½ teaspoon vanilla

- 1 ⅓ cup flour

- ½ teaspoon baking powder

- dash salt

- ½ cup crushed peanuts (optional)

Chocolate Chip Cookies

Ingredients:

- 1 cup butter
- ¾ cup brown sugar
- ½ cup white sugar
- 1 ½ teaspoons vanilla
- 1 egg
- 1 ¾ cups flour
- 1 teaspoon baking soda
- ½ teaspoon salt
- 1 cup chocolate chips

Method:

1. Preheat oven to 350°.

2. In a large mixing bowl, cream butter and sugars until light and fluffy.

3. Add egg and vanilla, beat until smooth.

4. Sift in flour, baking soda, and salt, and stir until everything is incorporated. Fold in chocolate chips.

5. Drop by the tablespoon onto a greased cookie sheet. Bake for 10 to 15 minutes until edges are golden but centres are still soft. Allow cookies to cool before transferring from cookie sheet to a wire cooling rack.

Lemon Blueberry Jam Bread

Method

1. Grease a loaf pan, Bundt pan, or 9 x 9 cake pan. To prevent formation of a thick crust, line the pan with parchment paper or tinfoil. Preheat oven to 350°.

2. Cream butter and sugar until light and fluffy. Add egg and vanilla and beat until smooth.

3. Add applesauce, lemon zest, and lemon juice. Stir.

4. Sift in dry ingredients. Mix until smooth.

5. In a separate bowl, place berries and sprinkle with 2 tablespoons of flour. Stir until all flour is absorbed, being careful not to crush the berries. This will help keep the berries from sinking in the batter. Gently fold floured berries into batter.

6. Pour into prepared pan and bake for 1 hour, or until cake tester comes out clean.

7. Serve warm with a dollop of lemon custard, blueberry jam, whipped cream, or ice cream.

Ingredients

- ¼ cup butter
- 1 cup brown sugar
- 1 egg
- 1 tablespoon vanilla
- ½ cup applesauce
- 2 tablespoons lemon zest
- 1 teaspoon lemon juice
- 2 cups flour
- 1 teaspoon baking soda
- ½ teaspoon salt
- ½ teaspoon nutmeg
- ½ teaspoon cinnamon
- 2 cups fresh blueberries
- 2 tablespoons flour

Autumn Apple Crisp

Ingredients

- 3 cups white flour

- 6 cups oatmeal

- 3 cups brown sugar

- ½ teaspoon cinnamon

- 2 cups butter, softened

- 5 pounds apples (McIntosh or Cortland), peeled, cored, and sliced

- ½ cup water

- ½ teaspoon cinnamon

Method

1. Preheat oven to 350°.

2. In a large bowl, sift together the flour, oatmeal, sugar, and cinnamon. Cut in butter. Stir until mixture resembles bread crumbs.

3. Press half of the mixture in the bottom of an ungreased 9 x 13 pan. Press firmly but do not pack down. Set aside.

4. Place apples in a deep pot over medium heat. Add water and cinnamon. Simmer, stirring often, until apples are half cooked, about 5 minutes.

5. Pour apple mixture onto crumb mixture. Loosely sprinkle with the rest of the crumb mixture.

6. Bake for 40 to 50 minutes until golden.

Serves 6–12

Cranberry Maple Pecan Tart

Method

1. Preheat oven to 350°.

2. Place pie dough in a lightly greased tart pan and sprinkle the dough with sugar.

3. Prepare Princess Cheesecake (recipe on page 162). Add maple syrup to the completed cheesecake batter, stirring until combined. Pour into the dough-lined pan.

4. Spread cranberries evenly over top and lightly press them into the batter. Sprinkle with the pecans and almonds, spreading them evenly across the berries. Press them so they are covered by some of the cheesecake batter to prevent burning.

5. Bake for 30 to 45 minutes until cheesecake is slightly firm.

Suggestion: For an added touch, drizzle finished tart with a chocolate or caramel sauce once cooled.

Makes 1 (9-inch) tart

Ingredients

> 1 Perfect Pie Crust (recipe on page 176)

> 2 tablespoons white sugar

> 1 Princess Cheesecake (recipe on page 162)

> ¼ cup maple syrup

> 2 cups fresh cranberries

> 1 cup pecans

> 1 cup almonds, sliced

Princess Cheesecake

Ingredients

- 2 (8-ounce) packages cream cheese, softened

- ½ cup sugar

- 2 tablespoons vanilla

- pinch of salt

- 2 eggs, room temperature

Method

1. Preheat oven to 350°.

2. In a deep bowl, stir cream cheese by hand or with a hand mixer until smooth, about 3 minutes.

3. Add sugar, vanilla, and salt. Stir.

4. Add eggs. Mix until smooth.

5. Prepare crust* and press into an 8-inch springform pan.

6. Pour batter into crust, smooth top with spatula.

7. Bake for 30 to 40 minutes, or until the edges are golden but the centre is still jiggly. Remove from oven and let sit until cool.

8. Refrigerate for 6 hours before removing cheesecake from pan.

*Variation: Try this cheesecake with a graham cracker crust (recipe on page 156), on shortbread, or with a gingersnap cookie crust (recipe on page 163).

Makes 1 (8-inch) cheesecake

Gingersnap Cookie Crust

This recipe can be used in place of the more traditional graham cracker crust for squares, bars, or cheesecakes.

Method

1. Crush cookies with a rolling pin or in food processor until they are fine crumbs.

2. In a mixing bowl, place cookie crumbs and butter, mixing until all butter is incorporated and mixture is crumbly.

3. Press into a pan and use as required.

4. Bake* at 325° for 12 to 15 minutes. Too long will result in a burnt cookie crust, so be careful!

*Hint: If you are preparing a recipe that calls for baking the dessert, there is no need to pre-cook the crust.

Makes 1 (9-inch) crust

Ingredients

- 2 cups gingersnap cookies

- 6 tablespoons butter, melted

Fruity Orange Dessert

Ingredients

- 2 cups seedless orange segments (fresh or canned)

- 1 cup yogurt (or puréed ricotta or cottage cheese)

- ½ cup orange juice

- ¼ cup orange-flavoured liqueur (Grand Marnier or Triple Sec)

- 1 teaspoon vanilla extract

- 2 cups ice cream, sherbert, or whipped cream

- ¼ cup chocolate chips, melted

Method

1. Lay orange segments in a spiral fashion on a dessert plate and set aside.

2. In a deep bowl, mix the yogurt or cheese with orange juice, liqueur, and vanilla until smooth.

3. Pour over orange segments, top with ice cream, sherbert, or whipped cream, then drizzle with chocolate.

Serves 4

Cold Fruit Salad

This salad makes a nice topping for ice cream too!

Method

1. Peel, rinse, and slice all fruit into bite-sized pieces.

2. In a large bowl, combine all fruit and add the cherry and lemon juices. Stir gently so as not to break or bruise the fruit.

3. Cover and refrigerate for 2 hours before using.

4. Serve with a side of whipped cream.

Serves 6–8

Ingredients

> 3 apples (Granny Smith or McIntosh)

> 2 Anjou pears

> 1 cup strawberries

> 1 banana

> ½ cup maraschino cherry juice

> ½ cup lemon juice

> 1 litre whipped cream

Toffee-Apple Oatmeal Pie

Ingredients

> 1 recipe Grandma's Classic Oatmeal Cookies (page 154)

> 3 cups Harvest Time Applesauce (recipe on page 168)

> 2 cups Skor bar, crushed into small pieces

> 1 (14-ounce) can sweetened condensed milk

Method

1. Preheat oven to 350°.

2. Prepare cookie recipe and press it gently into a 9 x 13 ungreased casserole dish.

3. Spread applesauce on top of cookie dough. Sprinkle evenly with Skor bits. Pour the sweetened condensed milk on top of everything.

4. Place casserole dish on a cookie sheet and bake until golden, about 30 to 45 minutes.

Variation: Try using blueberries, blueberry and applesauce mixed, pumpkin and applesauce mixed, pumpkin and cranberry mixed, or any variety that suits your taste buds.

Grandma's Baked Apples

Method

1. Preheat oven to 350°.

2. Pour apple juice into a shallow baking dish. Place cored apples in juice.

3. In a mixing bowl, prepare the Crumble Mixture. Add cinnamon and nutmeg and mix well.

4. Spoon the Crumble Mixture into the cored-out apples.

5. Bake until golden and juices bubble, about 20 to 45 minutes. Apples will be easy to pierce with a fork once tender.

6. Serve warm with whipped cream or ice cream.

Serves 4

Ingredients

- ½ cup apple juice

- 4 large apples (variety of choice but avoid soft apples like Red Delicious), washed and cored, peel on

- 1 Crumble Mixture (recipe on page 173)

- ½ teaspoon cinnamon

- ½ teaspoon nutmeg

Harvest Time Applesauce

Serve with whipped cream, on a hot breakfast cereal,
or as a condiment with lamb or pork dishes.

Ingredients

> 5 pounds apples* peeled,
  cored, and diced

> ½ cup water

> ½ teaspoon cinnamon

> dash of nutmeg

*Try adding some other fruit such as
pears, plums, peaches, apricots, blueberries, or cranberries.*

Method

1. Place all ingredients in a pot and stir well.

2. Cover and cook on low heat for 30 minutes stirring
   often, until fruit has become soft.

Hint: The longer you cook the apples the browner they
will become as the sugar in the apples caramelizes.
This highly concentrated applesauce is called apple
butter, and is sweeter than regular applesauce.

*Apple picking is a tradition as well as a livelihood for many
New Brunswickers. It's easy to get carried away at many
of the U-pick orchards and arrive home with more apples
than you can eat. Applesauce is the perfect answer for the
over-enthusiastic apple picker.*

Banana Flambé

Method

1. Slice bananas in half lengthwise and set aside.

2. In a nonstick frying pan, melt the butter and add water, cream, cranberry sauce, cherry juice, sugar, cherries, peppercorns, cinnamon, and clove.

3. Over medium heat, mix all until smooth.

4. Place one banana into the pan and cook for about 2 minutes on each side.

5. Add liqueur. Carefully ignite if desired; cover immediately to extinguish.

6. Remove banana from pan and plate.

7. Strain liquid through a fine sieve (discarding solid matter) and pour a little sauce over each banana.

8. Serve with ice cream or whipped cream, garnished with fresh berries.

Serves 1

Ingredients

> 1 ripe banana per person

> 1 tablespoon butter

> 2 tablespoon cold water

> 2 tablespoon heavy cream

> 2 tablespoon cranberry sauce

> ¼ cup cherry juice

> 1 tablespoon brown sugar

> 1 teaspoon maraschino cherries, minced

> ½ teaspoon whole black peppercorns

> dash cinnamon

> 1 clove

> 1 teaspoon liqueur of choice

> 1 cup berries for garnish*

Use your favourite berry or whatever is in season: strawberries, raspberries, blueberries, blackberries, etc.

Sweet Treats

Best Blueberry Muffins

This is a basic muffin recipe; to make another flavour simply omit the blueberries and substitute for another fruit (or chocolate chips).

Ingredients

- 1 cup blueberries*, rinsed

- 2 tablespoons flour

- 3 tablespoons melted butter

- ½ cup milk, slightly warmed

- 1 cup white sugar

- 2 eggs

- 1 teaspoon vanilla extract

- 1 ½ cups flour

- 2 teaspoons baking powder

- dash of salt

Method

1. Preheat oven at 375°.

2. In a mixing bowl, place berries and sprinkle with 2 tablespoons of flour. Stir until all flour is absorbed, being careful not to crush the berries. This will help keep the berries from sinking in the batter.

3. In a larger bowl, mix butter, milk, and sugar until smooth. Beat in eggs and vanilla.

4. Add dry ingredients. Stir until batter has no lumps. Gently fold in the blueberries.

5. Spoon into a greased muffin tin until ½ full.

6. Bake for 30 to 45 minutes, or until muffin tops spring back when pressed and cake tester comes out clean.

Variation: Cranberries, pineapple, apples, lemon zest, strawberries, may be used in place of, or in combination with, the blueberries.

Blueberry Grunt

Method

1. In a medium-sized pot combine berries, lemon juice, water, and sugar.

2. Cover and cook over low heat until consistency is jam-like, about 45 minutes.

3. Drop the dumpling dough into the jam. Push them about halfway under. Cover the pot, steam on low heat for about 15 minutes without lifting lid.

4. Serve warm dumplings with some of the jam sauce and cold whipped cream or ice cream.

Serves 4–8

Ingredients

> 4 cups fresh blueberries*

> 1 tablespoon lemon juice

> ¼ cup water

> ¼ cup white or brown sugar

> 1 recipe Dumplings (recipe on page 141).

> whipped cream or ice cream for garnish

*For variety try using a different fruit like strawberries, raspberries, plums, cranberries, etc.

Wild blueberries have been harvested for many generations in New Brunswick. Approximately 10 million pounds are produced annually by local farmers. August is the month of harvest, and berries cover fields and hillsides everywhere. Blueberries are sold fresh, frozen, and in any cooked form you can imagine.

Classic Banana Bread

Ingredients

- ¼ cup butter or margarine, softened

- 1 cup white sugar

- 1 egg

- 2 tablespoons peanut butter (optional)

- 3 bananas, peeled and mashed

- 1 ½ cups white flour

- 1 teaspoon baking soda

- ½ teaspoon salt

Method

1. Preheat oven to 350°. Grease a loaf pan. To prevent the formation of a thick crust, line the pan with parchment paper or tinfoil. Set aside.

2. In a large bowl, cream butter and sugar until light and fluffy. Add egg and peanut butter if using and beat until smooth.

3. Add bananas and mix well.

4. Add dry ingredients and stir until mixture is smooth.

5. Pour into prepared loaf pan and bake for 1 hour, or until cake tester comes out clean.

Hint: If top of loaf is getting too dark, gently lay a piece of tinfoil over top.

Crumble Mixture

Use this granola-like mixture as a topping on pies, cakes, muffins, or on apple crumble.

Method:

1. Preheat oven to 350°.

2. In a deep mixing bowl, combine oatmeal, flour, and brown sugar. Stir until even.

3. Cut in the butter, stirring until the mixture turns to a rough, lumpy dough and all the flour is absorbed. If the mixture is too sticky, add a bit more flour.

4. Spread onto an ungreased cookie sheet and bake for 15 minutes, or until mixture is crunchy and golden brown.

Ingredients:

> 1 cup oatmeal

> 1 cup flour

> ¾ cup brown sugar

> ½ cup butter, softened

Banana Supreme Cake

Ingredients:

> 1 banana bread (recipe on page 172)

> 1 (96-gram) box banana-flavoured instant pudding mix

> 1 Chocolate Chocolate Sauce (recipe on page 178)

> 1 ripe banana

> 1 cup whipped cream (optional)

Method:

1. Prepare Classic Banana Bread (recipe on page 172), but bake in two 8-inch pans (round or square).

2. Let the cakes cool, then dig out a shallow cavity in the centre of each one. Cut out about ¼ of the top of each cake, leaving a 1-inch border around the outside edge and the bottom intact. Set aside.

3. In a medium mixing bowl, prepare pudding according to package directions. Roughly chop banana bread pieces you scraped out from cakes. Add to pudding, cover, and refrigerate until firm.

4. On a cake plate, place one hollowed-out cake layer. Fill the cavity with half of the prepared pudding. Place second cake on top and repeat.

5. Slice the banana and place over top for decoration. Refrigerate cake for 20 minutes to set.

6. Prepare Chocolate Chocolate Sauce. Remove cake from fridge and pour sauce evenly over the top, allowing it to run down the sides of the cake. Serve immediately with a dollop of whipped cream.

Makes 1 (8-inch) double-layer cake

Bumbleberry Pie

Method:

1. Preheat oven to 425°.

2. In a deep mixing bowl, combine all berries and sprinkle with sugar, cinnamon, lemon juice, and salt. Stir until evenly coated and sugar is mostly dissolved.

3. Prepare pie plate by placing one crust in the bottom of an ungreased dish. Fill with berry mixture.

4. Sprinkle cornstarch evenly over the top of berry mixture.

5. Place second crust on top, pressing edges together and piercing a few holes in the top to allow pie to vent.

6. Bake 30 to 45 minutes, or until crust is golden and juices are bubbly.

Hint: Brush the top of your pie with an egg wash before baking for a beautiful golden and shiny crust. (Beat 1 egg with 1 tablespoon of cold water.) Sprinkle with a bit of white sugar for added crunch.

Makes 1 (9-inch) pie

Ingredients:

> 2 Perfect Pie Crust (recipe on page 176)

> 3 cups strawberries, hulled and sliced

> 3 cups blueberries

> 1 cup blackberries

> ½ cup brown sugar

> 1 teaspoon cinnamon

> 1 tablespoon lemon juice

> dash salt

> 3 tablespoons cornstarch

Perfect Pie Crust

Ingredients

> 2 cups flour

> ¾ cup shortening

> 1 teaspoon salt

> 4 to 8 tablespoons cold water

Method

1. Place flour in a deep bowl and cut in shortening with pastry cutter. Add salt and stir thoroughly until mixture resembles bread crumbs.

2. Gradually add the cold water (starting with just 2 tablespoons) until the dough forms a rough ball.

3. Wrap dough in plastic. Refrigerate for 20 minutes before using. If you flatten the ball slightly before wrapping, dough will be easier to roll out.

4. Uncooked dough will keep for 3 to 5 days in the fridge, or up to 4 months in the freezer.

5. Use as required. Generally, bake at 425° until golden brown.

Hint: The secret to good pie dough is not to handle it too much with your hands. Use a pastry cutter and wooden spoons to mix it, or use a food processor. Pulse in the processor until dough forms small roughly shaped balls, then gather into a big ball by hand before wrapping in plastic.

Makes 1 (9-inch) pie crust

Savoury Pie Crust

This crust is used mainly for meat pies. The cheese adds an extra touch of flavour to a savoury dish.

Method

1. In a large bowl, combine flour, cheese, and salt. Using a pastry cutter or 2 knives, cut in the butter and lard until the mixture resembles bread crumbs.

2. Gradually add water (1 tablespoon at a time), gently kneading, until the dough forms a rough ball.

3. Wrap dough in plastic. Refrigerate for 20 minutes before using. If you flatten the ball slightly before wrapping, dough will be easier to roll out.

4. Uncooked dough will keep for 3 to 5 days in the fridge, or up to 4 months in the freezer.

5. Use as required. Generally, bake at 425° until golden brown.

Makes 1 (9-inch) pie crust

Ingredients

- 1 ½ cups flour

- ½ cup sharp cheddar cheese, grated

- ½ teaspoon salt

- ⅓ cup cold butter

- ⅓ cup cold lard

- ¼ cup cold water

Chocolate Chocolate Sauce

Drizzle this delectable sauce over desserts and ice cream, or use as fondue.

Ingredients

- ⅔ cup icing sugar

- 2 tablespoons cocoa powder

- 1 teaspoon vanilla

- 3 to 4 teaspoons water

Method

1. Mix all in a bowl until smooth.

2. Store in refrigerator in an airtight jar for up to 1 month.

Makes approximately ⅔ cup

Blueberry-Maple Drizzle

This sauce is delicious hot or cold! Try it as a variation
on Maple-Glazed Chicken (recipe on page 28).

Method

1. In a medium saucepan, combine all ingredients and
   cook over low to medium heat for 20 minutes, stirring
   often.

2. Remove from heat and let cool for 5 minutes.

Makes approximately 5 cups

Ingredients

> 3 cups blueberries*

> 1 cup maple syrup

> 1 cup apple juice

> ¼ cup brown sugar

> 1 tablespoon vanilla extract

> ½ teaspoon cinnamon

*Instead of blueberries, try one or a
combination of the following flavours:
cranberry, raspberry, strawberry,
blackberry, or applesauce. Fruit can
be either jam, jelly, frozen (thaw first),
or freshly mashed.

Sweet Treats

The maple syrup season runs from early spring to early
summer. Take a tour of one of the many sugar shacks to
learn more about the harvesting and production of this
delicacy that makes many of our local desserts taste divine.

SAUCES

Rhubarb–Blackberry Chutney

Serve warm or cold over pancakes or potato latkes, or toss a spoonful over your favourite meat or vegetable dish.

Ingredients

- 6 cups rhubarb, thinly sliced

- 2 Granny Smith apples peeled, cored, and minced

- 1 cup sweet onion, minced

- ½ cup balsamic vinegar

- 1 teaspoon lemon zest

- ½ teaspoon allspice

- 1 teaspoon cracked black pepper

- pinch of salt

- 1 cup blackberries

Method

1. In a thick-bottomed saucepan, place all ingredients except the blackberries.

2. Simmer over low to medium heat until rhubarb is soft, approximately 30 to 60 minutes.

3. Once the rhubarb is softened, add blackberries and bring everything to a boil. Reduce heat immediately and simmer for 5 additional minutes.

Makes approximately 4 cups

Homespun Whipped Cream

Method

1. Using electric mixer, beat everything on highest setting until stiff peaks form, about 5 minutes.

2. Cover and refrigerate. You may need to re-beat before using if stored for a while. Will keep for up to 3 days.

Ingredients

> 4 cups whipping cream

> ½ cup icing sugar

> 1 teaspoon vanilla

When it comes time to get a Christmas tree, many tree farms offer a traditional family outing. You can ride out to find a tree on a wagon, then return to the cabin to warm up with delicious hot chocolate and gingerbread. Both taste better with a dollop of whipped cream.

Index